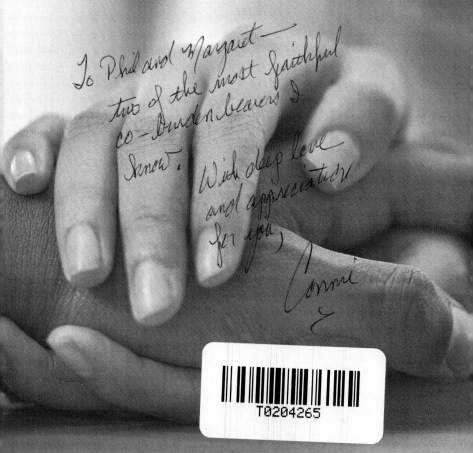

Pittsburgh Theological Seminary

Toward Bearing
One Another's Burdens

Praying with Others through
the Challenges of Life

To Phil and Margaret —
two of the most faithful
co-burden bearers I
know. With deep love
and appreciation
for you,

Connie

T0204265

Edited by
Connie Gundry Tappy

PITTSBURGH
THEOLOGICAL
SEMINARY

Pittsburgh Theological Seminary
616 N. Highland Ave.
Pittsburgh, PA 15206
412-362-5610
www.pts.edu

Editor: Connie Gundry Tappy
Designer: Melissa S. Logan

ISBN 978-0-9975924-1-2
Library of Congress Control Number: 2019908187

Contents

Editor's Preface

"O God, our Refuge in pain, our Strength in weakness,
our Help in trouble, our Solace in tears," we come to
Thee in our hour of need, beseeching Thee to have mercy
upon this Thine afflicted servant. . . . Let not his heart be
troubled, O Lord, but shed down upon him the peace
which passeth understanding. And, though now for a
season . . . he is in heaviness through his manifold trials,
yet comfort him, O Lord, in all his sorrows, and let his
mourning be turned into joy.[1]

So reads a 19th-century intercession uttered by churchman and Oxford
University professor E. B. Pusey and commended to pastors by then Bishop
of Wakefield William Walsham How. And today the task of all Christ-
followers to bear each other's burdens goes on.

In a 21st-century survey asking graduates of Pittsburgh Theological Seminary
what resources they would find helpful as they pursue their own varied
ministries, a request for a resource on prayer came to light—specifically, one
giving guidance on how to pray with and for people about difficulties that
arise throughout the course of life. *Toward Bearing One Another's Burdens*
responds to that request.

Faculty, program directors, and leaders from the Pittsburgh Seminary
community have here contributed essays on a wide range of topics to
assist people in thinking, acting, and speaking well in their work of helping
bear the burdens of others. These thoughtful essays do not give "correct"
answers on how all Christians should pray with all people undergoing very
specific, individual trials. The general guidance offered hinges on the giver's
theological perspective, Christian tradition, personal experience, and more.
And precisely because of the contributors' diversity of approach, readers
from a variety of viewpoints are likely to find contributions that speak to
their own needs for effective ministry.

The essays in this volume aim at helping Christian laypeople and leaders—
especially newer leaders—navigate theologically complicated issues with
the people to whom they minister. The compositions address topics by
answering such questions as:

---

[1] W. Walsham How, *Pastor in Parochiâ* (Gardner, Darton & Co., 1897), 85–86.

1. What is helpful to say/pray in a particular regard? What is unhelpful to say/pray, and why?

2. How can one incorporate Scripture in a prayer without becoming "preachy"?

3. Are there specific liturgies or prayers (individual or corporate) that might be quoted or consulted regarding the given difficulty?

4. What books, articles, and/or websites might one use or recommend for further consultation?

Preceded by introductory compositions on various aspects of prayer, the topical essays also point people to relevant biblical passages for discerning how God's word might further shape a person's caring for people facing difficult challenges. The quotations from Scripture contained in the essays come from the New Revised Standard Version of the Bible, copyright 1989, by the Division of Christian Education of the National Council of Churches of Christ in the U.S.A.

A blank page for jotting down notes follows each topical essay. For ease of reference, the sample prayers at the end of each composition also appear as an excerpted group at the end of the volume.

May this resource help Christians in all parts of our broken world heed the call to "Bear one another's burdens, and in this way . . . fulfill the law of Christ" (Gal. 6:2).

Connie Gundry Tappy
Senior Writer
Pittsburgh Theological Seminary

Introductory Essays

"The Spirit helps us in our weakness; for we
do not know how to pray as we ought, but
that very Spirit intercedes with sighs too deep
for words. And God, who searches the heart,
knows what is the mind of the Spirit, because
the Spirit intercedes for the saints according
to the will of God."

— Romans 8:26–27 —

Prayer According to Biblical and Traditional Teaching

Christians who desire to pray for and with people aspire to a noble calling: the Apostle Paul teaches us to "pray without ceasing," and Jesus instructed us even to "pray for those who persecute you." But knowing the importance of prayer and living a life of prayer are two different things. In the Bible, prayer is taught both by precept and by example. That our omnipotent God invites—indeed, commands—us to pray is in itself astonishing! What can we offer of which he has any need? The invitation that God issues brings us into his own counsel and dignifies human beings, who have been made after his image and likeness. In the command to pray, along with the original command to tend this world and to be fruitful and multiply, we are being embraced by the very life of God, who is all bountiful, and from whom all life and blessing flows. In prayer, we echo the communal mystery of the Trinity, of the God who said, "*Let us* make Adam [a human being, humankind] in our image," and who then made humankind male and female, in community, to reason and talk with one another. Prayer is the sign that we share in the very life and will of the Triune God!

Throughout the Old Testament we see numerous models of godly prayer: the righteous Abraham, who prayed on behalf of Sodom and Gomorrah; Moses, who interceded for rebellious Israel; David, who prayed for forgiveness; the seraphim, who, in Isaiah 6, adore God with the address "Holy! Holy! Holy!"; Hannah, who prayed earnestly for a child; Hezekiah, who repented on behalf of Israel and thus averted the Assyrian scourge; Ezra, who called on his people to rededicate themselves to the Lord; and the Maccabean martyrs with their mother (traditionally called "Solomonia"), who asked God for courage to withstand torture.

Throughout the New Testament, examples also abound, from Anna, who spent her whole life in the Temple and translated devotion into a prophetic word about the Messiah, to the final word of the visionary John, who cries out with mother Church, "Even so, Come Lord Jesus!" (where Lord associates Jesus, the Incarnate God, with Yhwh, the "I am" of the Old Testament; cf. 1 Cor. 8:6). But of course our clearest example of prayer is given in Jesus. At every moment, he is in communion with the Father; at every crucial occasion, he is reported as praying; even at the very moment of his death, he asks the Father to bless those who are crucifying him.

From Jesus, too, we receive the prayer pattern of the perfect human being, who shows us how to be in communion with the Father and with others. Reciting The Lord's Prayer is a helpful and calming practice when we are in distress or do not know how to pray, for in doing so we "dress up" as the Son (as C. S. Lewis put it) and so become more and more like him. In praying as he taught us to do, we can be sure that the Holy Spirit is praying in us and that our prayers are pleasing to God. In reciting The Lord's Prayer we name God as Father; we hallow and adore him; we anticipate his final fulfillment of the creation; we pray that his will be done even now, before that great Day; we request our daily needs (and those of others) in confidence; we ask for forgiveness and extend it to others; we recognize our need for his help in times of temptation and trial at the hands of his enemy, whose days are numbered. Prayer according to this pattern becomes a time of worship, consolation, and spiritual warfare. Beyond merely reciting this prayer, we can use it as a kind of template for organizing our more personal prayers around each of its clauses. In this way, we give structure and discipline to our prayer while also making room for our particular circumstances.

But prayer is not magic, of course. Prayer with integrity must match the whole of our lives, and effective prayer is something we must prepare for with every breath! There will be times that are too urgent or too confusing for words; as with any crisis, it is then that our "spiritual instincts" must take over, and even in our wordlessness we can know that the Holy Spirit prays in each one of us and among us as a body (Rom. 8:22ff.). In my own life, I have found it helpful to practice not only specific times devoted to the Lord in prayer—a rule of prayer organized around The Lord's Prayer, other traditional prayers, and biblical meditation—but also to pray throughout the day the little phrase known as the "Jesus Prayer": "Lord Jesus Christ, Son of God, have mercy on me, a sinner." This prayer is directly drawn from the Gospels and amplified by the acknowledgment of one's own sins before the Lord and others. When I consciously pray this phrase, I try to match my in-taken breath to "Lord Jesus Christ, Son of God," and my exhaled breath to "have mercy on me, a sinner," thus breathing in the life of the God-Man and breathing out my sin and confusion. When I *constantly* pray this prayer, it settles in the background of my life and blessedly emerges from under the surface of my consciousness at times when I need to remember God's presence. The Jesus Prayer is a faithful companion for me in times of boredom, concern, struggle, and the whole daily routine. Moreover, this prayer, along with The Lord's Prayer, has been beloved for centuries. Praying it enlivens my awareness of being surrounded by the "cloud of witnesses" continually praying for me.

It seems that we need both *formal* prayer and *constant* prayer, and it is The Lord's Prayer and The Jesus Prayer that many Christians have found helpful in maintaining both practices. But we must not become discouraged or guilt-ridden when establishing a rule of prayer and being continually aware of God's presence do not come naturally or consistently—for the Lord's will for us is simply to turn to him again and again as we become increasingly aware of our needs and of his deep love for us and others. Neither, however, should we become lazy about prayer, for it is only when prayer becomes natural to us (despite our weaknesses) that we can pray for others without a sense of self-consciousness or artificiality. Once both formal prayer and constant prayer become natural and inevitable parts of our daily routine, we can draw on many other biblical and traditional prayers to nurture and deepen our communion with the Lord and with other Christians, both on earth and in heaven.

On behalf of Jesus' disciples, one of them requested of the Lord, "teach us [how] to pray" (Luke 11:1). Jesus taught them—and us—via his example of and template for prayer. But the instruction continues as the Holy Spirit of God, praying within us, teaches us what to say, when to be silent, and when to listen.[2] In this partnership with God (2 Cor. 9:1) we are lifted to his glory, yet we remain always the junior members.

Dr. Edith M. Humphrey
William F. Orr Professor of New Testament

---

[2] Contemporary readers may find helpful guidance in Morton T. Kelsey's *The Other Side of Silence: Meditation for the Twenty-First Century* (Paulist, 1997).

PRAYER AS A GIFT OF THE SPIRIT

Though the New Testament epistles were written to particular Christian communities, the letters do not explicitly list prayer among the spiritual gifts they enumerate (see Rom. 12:1–8; 1 Cor. 12; Eph. 4:1–16; 1 Pet. 4:10-11). The letters do address the communities' particular circumstances, however. In his first letter to the church in Corinth, for example, Paul corrects the misuse of a series of spiritual gifts and the division that ensued from certain community members' prideful disregard for the gifts of other members. Certainly, we know there are many good gifts of the Holy Spirit—gifts that proclaim Jesus as Lord and serve the common life of the Spirit-formed community are spiritual gifts (see 1 Cor. 12:3, 7; Eph. 4:12–13, 16). But while as individuals we receive spiritual gifts that differ from the gifts given to others ("For as in one body we have many members, and not all the members have the same function," Rom. 12:4), the Holy Spirit freely gives the gift of prayer to each one of us.

Still, we may observe that some people are particularly gifted at praying in a certain manner or in certain circumstances (many of which are discussed in the contents of this resource). But regardless of one's sense of confidence or ability in praying with and for others, the gift of prayer is indeed given to all those who bear the name "Christian." It is the gift of relationship with the God who promises to be with us in all the circumstances of life. It is the gift of Christ's transforming work through the Holy Spirit in our hearts, minds, and very being. It is the gift of becoming increasingly Christ-like as God builds the heavenly kingdom here in our midst.

> I appeal to you therefore, brothers and sisters, by the mercies of God, to present your bodies as a living sacrifice, holy and acceptable to God, which is your spiritual worship. Do not be conformed to this world, but be transformed by the renewing of your minds, so that you may discern what is the will of God—what is good and acceptable and perfect (Rom. 12:1–2).

In her book *Christian Prayer for Today*, Martha Moore-Keish puts it this way: ". . . prayer is not our triumphant ability to address God directly. It is the Holy Spirit's work in and through us. In this way, prayer itself is a gift of God."[3] We know from the scriptural discourses on spiritual gifts that misuse of such gifts causes division and conflict rather than unity and edification.

---

[3] Martha Moore-Keish, *Christian Prayer for Today* (Westminster John Knox, 2009), 82.

What we do and say is right and true only when it is in accordance with God's will. Prayer is given in the aid of such alignment. It is the gift not necessarily of knowing God's will, but of the opportunity to be guided and shaped by it nonetheless.

While some aspects of God's will are clearly revealed to us in Scripture, much of God's will remains hidden from us. In many of life's circumstances we struggle to discern what God wants, what will most fully glorify Christ in and through us. "And this is the boldness we have in him, that if we ask anything according to his will, he hears us. And if we know that he hears us in whatever we ask, we know that we have obtained the requests made of him" (1 John 5:14–15).

How then do we pray if we do not know God's will? How do we pray when faced with a challenging decision in which someone will inevitably be hurt? For what do we pray when we find ourselves in physically or emotionally dangerous territory and do not know whether to seek release or perseverance? The answer: Since God knows his own heart, the Spirit intercedes for us. The Spirit who hovered over the waters at creation and brought life and beauty out of chaos; the Spirit who raised Jesus from the dead and raises us to new life; the Spirit who was poured out upon humanity at Pentecost in order that the ascended Lord would fill all things—it is by this Spirit that we are encouraged and empowered to pray. By this Spirit, our deepest needs are brought before God. And by this Spirit, God's will is transcribed on our hearts. It is through the gift of prayer that God's will shapes us such that our hearts and minds become aligned with God's desire and will.

This reality is the reason we pastors turn to God in prayer as we prepare sermons—and even just before preaching them. We know that any faithful, wise, and prophetic word we might offer comes not from our own insightful intellect, but from God. And we know that in our imperfection, we need the Holy Spirit to take control both of the words we speak from the pulpit and the ears of those who sit in the pews, in order that God's word might truly be proclaimed. Without prayer, our words are empty. Thus the gift of prayer is essential to the exercise of preaching—in fact, to the exercise of all pastoral gifts and spiritual gifts of all kinds.

> But if we hope for what we do not see, we wait for it with patience. Likewise the Spirit helps us in our weakness; for we do not know how to pray as we ought, but that very Spirit intercedes with sighs too deep for words. And God, who searches the heart, knows what is the mind of the

Spirit, because the Spirit intercedes for the saints according to the will of God (Rom. 8:25–27).

It is the Holy Spirit within us who enables us to pray. And more, it is the Holy Spirit who empowers us to pray rightly. According to John Calvin, the Spirit "arouses in us assurances, desires, and sighs, to conceive which our natural powers would scarcely suffice."[4] Calvin points out that we hardly know what to say to God. Certainly we experience a great deal of unspeakable tragedy in this broken world. In the face of such tragedy, we have no answers; therefore, we turn to God. But our lack of answers also means that at times we don't even know what petitions to offer. In our weakness, the Spirit prays for God to enact the circumstances that would most fully glorify Christ in and through us. "Clearly, then, to pray rightly is a rare gift."[5] Praying rightly shapes our perception of ourselves, the world, and God. As we pray, the Spirit moves in our hearts to elicit an increasingly Christ-like response to the world around us. "Pray in the Spirit at all times in every prayer and supplication. To that end keep alert and always persevere in supplication for all the saints [i.e., God's people]" (Eph. 6:18).

According to Karl Barth,

> it is not possible to say "I shall pray" or "I shall not pray," as if it were an act according to our own good pleasure. To be a Christian and to pray are one and the same thing; it is a matter that cannot be left to our caprice. It is a need, a kind of breathing necessary to life.[6]

For we are never separated from God, and God is never separated from us. Our very being rests in God's free grace, and our prayers proceed from that same grace. This gift of prayer is part and parcel of our identity as a people who, through the waters of baptism and in the power of the Holy Spirit, have been claimed as Christ's own, cast into the presence of the Father, and given eternal relationship with the Triune God—a gift of the Spirit indeed.

The Rev. Kendra L. Buckwalter Smith '12/'13
Director of the Worship Program

---

[4] John Calvin, *Institutes of the Christian Religion* (ed. John T. McNeill; trans. Ford Lewis Battles; Westminster John Knox, 1960), 855. N.B. In 1968, Dr. Ford Lewis Battles, a Rhodes Scholar and respected academician best known for his study and translations of writings by leaders of the Protestant Reformation, joined the faculty of Pittsburgh Theological Seminary as professor of church history and doctrine.
[5] Calvin, *Institutes*, 856.
[6] Karl Barth, *Prayer* (ed. Don E. Saliers; Westminster John Knox, 2002), 15.

Prayer as a Spiritual Discipline

In his book *Celebration of Discipline*, Richard Foster writes, "Of all the Spiritual Disciplines prayer is the most central because it ushers us into perpetual communion with the Father."[7] Spiritual disciplines are activities we engage in (or refrain from, as in fasting) to train our bodies, minds, and spirits to be more Christ-like. They are profitable for us not as practices to be mastered for their own sake, but as tools to increase our capacity to appropriate God's grace and to enable us to live more deeply, fully, and frequently under God's reign.

Dallas Willard describes how young people who idolize certain professional sports figures will try to mimic through posture, movement, equipment, and dress whatever their favorite star does in the hope of being like him or her when they play the star's game. Willard remarks, however, that the "exquisite responses we see" as the star performs on the field or court "are available to the athlete for those short and all-important hours because of a daily regimen no one sees."[8] Similarly for Christians, when urgent needs arise we desire to be able to pray with the power of saints, whether they be renowned figures from the Church's storied past or respected pastors, friends, or relatives in our own time—our persistently prayerful grandmother, for example. Almost instinctively, in our prayers we want to respond with the right attitude, right words, and right amount of faith, all of which require engaging in a regimen of learning, training, and practice.

As Christians seeking to follow Jesus, we know we are to pattern our lives with the disciplines he modeled for us, including prayer. The Gospel of Mark tells us that, early in the Lord's ministry, after a highly successful night of healing people in Capernaum, Jesus withdrew to a "deserted place" to pray, likely to seek counsel and strength from God for the new day's tasks of further preaching and healing (Mark 1:35–39). From Luke we learn that Jesus did so regularly—as the crowds' demands on him grew, "he would withdraw to deserted places and pray" (Luke 5:16). Luke also reveals that Jesus prayed before making significant decisions, such as naming his apostles (Luke 6:12–16), revealing his identity to them (Luke 9:18, 28), and accepting his death on the cross (Luke 22:41–44). If Jesus regularly needed to withdraw from all the demands of his life to spend time alone with God for counsel and strength, especially when facing important turning points and difficulties, how much more do we, his followers, need to do so.

---

[7] Richard Foster, *Celebration of Discipline: The Path to Spiritual Growth* (rev. ed.; Harper Collins, 1988), 33.
[8] Dallas Willard, *The Spirit of the Disciplines: Understanding How God Changes Lives* (Harper & Row, 1988), 4.

There are many ways to engage in the discipline of prayer. One might learn about praying by studying the prayers in Scripture, perhaps beginning with The Lord's Prayer or some of the prayers of Paul (e.g., Col. 1:9–14; Eph. 1:15–23; 3:14–21). Memorizing such biblical prayers and/or personalizing them by adding our own names or those of loved ones affords us the opportunities to practice engaging in these Spirit-filled words and to train our minds and consciousness toward greater awareness of spiritual realities. Additionally, singing hymns, spiritual songs, or even some secular favorites may help facilitate our expressing our thoughts and emotions to God. St. Augustine is credited with saying, "Those who sing, pray twice."

In his book *Prayer: Finding the Heart's True Home*, Richard Foster offers a primer on 21 types of prayer. He groups them into three categories: moving inward, seeking the transformation we need; moving upward, seeking the intimacy we need; and moving outward, seeking the ministry we need. Foster helps readers to understand, experience, and practice prayer in its mutlivarious forms. The many classic works on prayer include Andrew Murray's *With Christ in the School of Prayer*, Thomas Merton's *Contemplative Prayer*, and Teresa of Ávila's *Interior Castle*. My own Anglican tradition commends praying the Daily Office as a spiritual discipline—it includes Bible reading and set prayers. This practice forms our minds and spirits into certain patterns of thought so that, in time, the prayers we pray regularly pray within us and provide a lens through which we see the world, thus shaping us and our responses to what we encounter in daily life.

In its essence, prayer is communication with God. Human communication happens through many forms—primarily the use of words, spoken or written, but not exclusively. Anyone who has observed two people who love each other deeply—a couple married for many years, a mother with her newborn infant—can easily perceive the dialogue that takes place between them without a word's being spoken. So it can be between God and us in prayer. Sometimes we can gaze at God's beauty through the created order and simply sigh our thanksgivings for the wonder we feel surrounding and upholding us. Amid terrible trauma and shock, we may not be able to utter words or even begin to know where to start to voice our concerns. St. Paul writes of the Spirit's helping us in our times of weakness when we do not know how or what to pray—of the Spirit's interceding with sighs and groans that words cannot express, all in accordance with God's will (Rom. 8:26–27).

When developing the practice of prayer as a spiritual discipline, experimenting with various forms, methods, and ways of praying is to be encouraged; but persisting with each means of prayer for enough time truly to evaluate its worth and effects on the pray-er's life is at least equally important. To do so, you might want to ask yourself, "What is it about my spirit that needs to be disciplined or trained?" Perhaps the first step in answering that question is taking stock of your prayer life to assess your starting points, strengths, weaknesses, etc. Be honest with yourself and ask God to help you set an agenda or training regimen to nurture your growth into the prayerful person you sense God calling you to be. You might benefit from consulting with a trained spiritual director to help identify which types of prayer fit your personality and spiritual background. You might ask people whose prayerfulness you admire how they have been trained and formed in prayer and what practical means they have found useful and necessary to remaining faithful in this discipline.

Finally, as you develop and nurture prayer as a spiritual discipline in your life, be aware that prayer is primarily a transformational rather than a transactional activity. In a world that proclaims, "You get what you pay for!" those who pray learn that "you *become* what you pray for." As Richard Foster writes, "To pray is to change. Prayer is the central avenue God uses to transform us. If we are unwilling to change, we will abandon prayer as a noticeable characteristic of our lives."[9]

The Rev. Dr. Catherine M. Brall
Director of Field Education

---

[9] Foster, *Celebration of Discipline*, 33.

Prayer as a Conversation

Imagine you're hanging out with friends, just talking and having a good time until someone breaks the natural flow of the conversation to ask whether you're doing it right. Really? Do our conversations have checklists to follow? Is there a required format for talking with friends? A sure way to kill a conversation is to ask about its structure. Have we told enough stories? Asked for advice? Complained about sports teams? Told a few jokes?

Sure, we often do all these things in a conversation. But we do them best when we're being spontaneous, not when we're thinking hard and planning the next thing we're going to say. Thinking stops the conversation.

Prayer is conversation. John Calvin speaks of it as a conversation with God. Or as Jürgen Moltmann says, "God listens to his friends." Then he adds: "Friendship with God finds its preeminent expression in prayer."[10] And just as too much thinking stops a conversation with friends, too much theologizing stops our conversation with God.

When we think about prayer, then, let us think about God. Think about how Jesus prayed often, or how he invites followers to "watch and pray." Think about the risen Christ who prays for us continually, thus bearing our prayers to the very heart of God. Think about the Spirit whom Christ sends, and stay fixed on the promise of the Spirit until you can stop merely thinking and start actually awakening to the gentle presence within—a holy presence that is energizing you like your pulse or your breath, only closer to you than any part of you. Awaken to the presence, and your prayer will be natural.

We fail to pray because we fail to sense God's presence. When God is real, prayer is spontaneous, joyous, and free. It flows without thinking, like conversation with friends. We long for the practice of spontaneous prayer—the kind that breaks out within us, as unexpected as a burst of sunshine which comes even before the rain stops! For spontaneity like the cry of a toddler suddenly alone, a cry that is utterly honest and uncontrived. Like a flock of birds startled into flight. A gasp of joy, perhaps, or fear, our deepest and most honest feelings expressed in real time to our kindest and most faithful friend. A shudder over a fear unknown, a spontaneous upsurge of inarticulate feeling, "sighs too deep for words" (Rom. 8:26).

---

[10] Jürgen Moltmann, *The Trinity and the Kingdom of God* (Fortress, 1993), 221.

Yes, of course, prayer has moments of thanksgiving and praise, pleading and petition, intercession on behalf of others, and times of quiet listening. And certainly it is appropriate to *think* about our prayer life, to take it seriously—to take the truly awesome privilege of communicating with God seriously! But our conversations with God do not have to follow a rigid checklist, a fixed pattern or structure, and definitely not a theological agenda of categories that have to be checked off. Certainly it is good to express our gratitude for the blessings of the new day, for example. But immediately upon doing so we may become mindful of people entrapped in poverty, sickness, or violence. So let our prayers shift naturally to focus on those hardships and on other concerns, joys, petitions, and more as God's Spirit directs. For in prayer, joy and sorrow mix in our hearts, as they must in God's own heart.

By ending each day in conversation with God, we entrust our going to sleep to the One who keeps watch without slumber. We let the day go. And in that moment between wakefulness and sleep, we experience joy, wonder, calm, regret, forgiveness, peace, and healing, somehow all flowing together in one prayerful moment of release. As we let go our sins, our pride, our very self, we feel unburdened, more aware of God and less aware of self, by calmly putting down life's little day in order to enter more fully into the mystery of the Day that lies ahead.

We pray when we sense that God is real and present. We sense that God is real and present because we pray. Circular, of course, but that's how it is with any conversation. Conversations make friends, and friends make conversations. So it is with prayer. God is listening. And waiting.

Let the conversation begin.

The Rev. Dr. Ron S. Cole-Turner
H. Parker Sharp Professor of Theology and Ethics

Topical Essays

"Where two or three are gathered in my
name, I am there among them."

— Matthew 18:20 —

"And this is the boldness we have in him,
that if we ask anything according to his will,
he hears us."

— 1 John 5:14 —

Abuse Suffered (Physical and Emotional)

Abuse of any kind is a profound violation of an individual's dignity and personhood. People who have suffered this kind of trauma may find it difficult to reconcile their experiences with their faith. For this reason, praying with a survivor of abuse requires special attentiveness and care. Although it is crucial to help those who have suffered abuse to find the psychological and emotional support they need from trained professionals, it is equally important to address survivors' spiritual needs, such as acceptance within the faith community and assurance of God's love.

People who have experienced abuse may carry with them a deep sense of shame, or even a fear that they may be "unlovable." One helpful approach for praying with such individuals may be to pray in ways that assure them they are cherished children of God, that God is present with them in their suffering, and that nothing can separate them from God's love. Scripture passages that might be helpful in this regard include Psalms 23, 46, and 139, as well as Romans 8:37–39:

> In all things we are more than conquerors through him who loved us. For I am convinced that neither death, nor life, nor angels, nor rulers, nor things present, nor things to come, nor powers, nor height, nor depth, nor anything else in all creation, will be able to separate us from the love of God in Christ Jesus our Lord.

Some survivors of abuse may also have strong feelings of anger or sadness about what they have been through. They may feel the need to lament, cry out, or even rail at God as a way of processing what has happened to them. Here again the Psalms may be particularly helpful, as they express such a wide range of human emotions. For example, Psalms 35, 69, and 77 may help give voice to the complex feelings of grief, rage, desperation, and hope that survivors of abuse may experience.

Pastoral caregivers working with survivors of abuse should be very careful around the topic of forgiveness. Suggesting that a survivor pray to forgive his or her abuser could circumvent the healing process and/or reinforce feelings of guilt or shame if the person does not yet feel ready to forgive. Focusing too quickly on forgiveness might also send the message that the abuser's behavior wasn't that bad, or that the abuser should not be held accountable.

Similarly, when praying with survivors of abuse, it is important to be mindful of language related to suffering. Be careful not to pray in a way that suggests the suffering is deserved, or that God somehow engineered the suffering as a way of "teaching you a lesson." Such interpretations of suffering are usually not helpful and may actually make a survivor's feelings of despair even worse. Instead, other theological themes—such as the hope of the resurrection, God's abiding presence, or the goodness of God's creation—will likely feel more supportive to someone who has suffered the pain of abuse.

Perhaps most important to remember if you are called upon to pray with a survivor of abuse is to be as fully present as you can be, even if you feel anxious or uncomfortable. Try to listen to what the person is expressing without judging or attempting to "fix" the problem. Assure the person you are ministering to that he or she is a beloved child of God and that God does not wish for anyone to suffer in this way. Pray for healing, for peace, and for the individual to sense God's presence even in the midst of very challenging circumstances.

You might consider using a prayer such as this one:

Gracious God, we thank you for your deep, deep love for your whole creation, and for all your people, who are made in your image. This day, we pray especially for your beloved child, _____ (name). Help _____ (name) to sense your tender care, even in the midst of very difficult circumstances. With thanks for your abiding presence we pray. Amen.

The Rev. Dr. Leanna K. Fuller
Associate Professor of Pastoral Care

Helpful resources for further consultation include:

> "Prayer for Healing Victims of Abuse," from the United States Conference of Catholic Bishops: http://www.usccb.org/prayer-and-worship/prayers-and-devotions/prayers/prayer-for-healing-victims-of-abuse.cfm;

> "Prayer for Survivors," from *Survivor Today* online magazine: https://survivortoday.org/2013/07/28/prayer-for-survivors/;

"Prayers for Survivors: A Liturgy in Protest of Sexual Violence," from StrongWomenWrite: https://strongwomenwrite.wordpress.com/tag/prayers-for-survivors-of-abuse/; and

We Were the Least of These: Reading the Bible with Survivors of Sexual Abuse, by Elaine A. Heath (Brazos, 2011).

NOTES

Addiction and Substance Abuse

Addiction is a disease of the body, mind, and spirit. It is also America's leading killer when you consider smoking (nicotine) as a form of addiction leading to cancer and lung and heart disease. Overdoses of alcohol and drugs now comprise the leading cause of death for people under the age of 50. America is in an "addiction epidemic," as recognized by the Surgeon General and even declared by the President of the United States as a "national emergency." What are we as Christians to do to help those afflicted by this disease? We are called to love, to teach, and to heal!

What is addiction? The word addiction comes from classical Latin, with *ad* meaning "to" or "toward" and *dicere* meaning "to speak." According to Roman law, a person became an *addictus* when he/she was handed over formally in accordance with a judicial decision. In other words, when one becomes an addict, he/she is turned over to another power. The person addicted to alcohol and/or drugs has become controlled by the substance(s).

As a disease, addiction has symptoms, such as denial, obsession, and compulsion. In the process of denial, the addict loses touch with reality. The addicted person believes he/she is free to choose to use or not use alcohol or other drugs when, in fact, he/she has become enslaved to them and is therefore unable to choose freely. Obsession stems from the mental process that causes an addicted person to spend more and more of his/her mental energy thinking about and finding means to obtain the addicting substance(s). Addicted persons become preoccupied with "using" to the extent that their life becomes ever narrower as it centers increasingly on that goal and activity. Compulsion is the result of a person's using a chemical or substance—it starts a phenomenon of craving. As the ancient saying goes, "A man takes a drink; the drink takes a drink; the drink takes the man."

When working with and caring for addicted persons, we ourselves must realize that we are powerless over the process of addiction. We can help addicted people by sending them to detox to remove the toxin or poison from their body, thus addressing the physical aspect of addiction. But since addiction is a disease of the body, mind, and spirit, we must also address the mental compulsion that leads people back to the poison once again. Therapy, support groups, and 12-Step programs are therefore essential to addicts' breaking out of the prison of isolation they find themselves in as their addiction grows and worsens.

Finally, the spiritual dimension of addiction must be addressed. As is often heard at 12-Step meetings, "If you are not praying, you are not staying!" Praying for and with the addicted person—and family members who have been affected by the disease of addiction—is the bedrock of recovery. Prayer is the beginning of hope. It is the foundation of spiritual rebirth. As Jesus declares in Matthew 7:24–25,

> Everyone then who hears these words of mine and does them will be like a wise man who built his house on rock. And the rain fell, and the floods came, and the winds blew and beat on that house, but it did not fall, because it had been founded on rock.

The acrostic, mnemonic phrase DOCTOR can be a helpful tool when working with those who are addicted:

D = Denial
O = Obsession
C = Compulsion
T = Treatment
O = Ongoing
R = Recovery

Denial, obsession, and compulsion are the main symptoms of addiction we must help addicted persons see in themselves in order to help them find treatment and ongoing recovery. Like diabetes, for example, addiction is a lifelong illness that demands a change in lifestyle in order for the sufferer to become well—indeed, even to survive. Like evil, addiction does not simply vanish, never to return: as the Apostle Peter proclaims, "Discipline yourselves, keep alert. Like a roaring lion your adversary the devil prowls around, looking for someone to devour" (1 Pet. 5:8).

A prayer that is often heard in 12-Step rooms is the shortened version of the Serenity Prayer. Recite and repeat this prayer often when you are working with and helping those who are addicted or affected by the ravages of addiction. Many people who know the shortened version of the Serenity Prayer are unaware of the longer version (below), written by theologian Reinhold Niebuhr. May this prayer help you as you pray with people who are addicted—and, most of all, help the addicted persons themselves!

God grant me the serenity to accept the things I cannot change; courage to change the things I can; and wisdom to know the difference. Living one day at a time; enjoying one moment at a time; accepting hardships as the pathway to peace; taking, as He did, this sinful world as it is, not as I would have it; trusting that He will make all things right if I surrender to His Will; that I may be reasonably happy in this life and supremely happy with Him forever in the next. Amen.

The Rev. Canon Dr. William (Jay) Geisler '99
Canon for Ordained Vocations and Chaplain to the Mon Valley
Mission Initiative, Episcopal Diocese of Pittsburgh

Helpful resources for further consultation include:

> *Addiction and Grace: Love and Spirituality in the Healing of Addictions*, by Gerald G. May (reissue ed.; HarperOne, 2007);

> *Breathing Under Water: Spirituality and the Twelve Steps*, by Richard Rohr O.F.M. (Franciscan Media, 2011);

> *God Loves the Addict: Experiencing Recovery on the Path of Grace*, by Eddie Snipes (CreateSpace, 2013);

> *Save Me from Myself: How I Found God, Quit Korn, Kicked Drugs, and Lived to Tell My Story*, by Brian Welch (HarperOne, 2009);

> https://www.addictioncenter.com/community-resources/;

> https://www.drugabuse.gov/publications/principles-drug-addiction-treatment-research-based-guide-third-edition/resources; and

> https://www.publichealth.org/resources/addiction/.

NOTES

ADOPTION

"(God) destined us for adoption as his children through Jesus Christ, according to the good pleasure of his will, to the praise of his glorious grace that he freely bestowed on us in the Beloved" (Eph. 1:5–6). Kinship by blood (my parents, children, siblings, cousins, etc.) and kinship by marriage (my spouse, in-laws, sisters-in-law, etc.) form the warp and woof of the basic unit of human society, the family. Around the world, every society has developed an intricate system of rules and customs to govern questions of lineage ("To whom am I related?"), inheritance ("Who will care for my children and my possessions after I die?"), marriage ("What rights and obligations do I acquire by publicly binding myself to my partner?"), and other such questions.

But in this sea of rules, there is an exception: adoption (from the Latin *ad*, "toward," and *option*, "choice"). Breaking with the regular rules of kinship by blood and marriage, adoption creates a new category in which an adult chooses a child, thus conferring on that child all the rights, privileges, and inheritance normally reserved for biological children. Though the adopted child has done nothing to deserve this outpouring of gracious benevolence—potentially lands, title, reputation, prestige, wealth, and even the right to be sibling with the parent's/s' biological children—the act is binding and irreversible, and the adopted child's life is forever changed. And in the biblical narrative, it is clear that the decision to adopt a child is extremely important to that child's identity and well-being.

In these times of increased numbers of orphaned and needy children but a decreasing number of domestic and international adoptions in the United States, there remain three main ways that U.S. citizens welcome children into their homes through adoption: private adoption, adoption through the foster care system, and international adoption. Private adoption and international adoption have declined significantly over the past decade or so, and international adoption has seen significant increases in cost and administrative safeguards. Adoption through the foster care system is more complex today due to the ongoing challenges to that system: transracial adoption and the adoption of children with trauma issues have added complexity but also respond to critical needs.

Pastors are often consulted by church members on a range of issues concerning adoption, including psychological, ethical, spiritual, and practical questions. Perhaps the three most helpful ways a pastor can prepare to respond to such questions are:

1. Offer to listen to and pray with an individual or couple considering adoption. God calls certain individuals to open their lives to an adopted child, but as Proverbs 19:2 observes, "Desire without knowledge is not good," or as some translations put it, "zeal without wisdom is foolishness." There are few decisions that will more profoundly affect the life of the child and the church member than the decision to adopt. Providing a safe space where members considering adoption can begin to discern their own hopes and limitations is extremely important. Are they open to adopting transracial, special needs, or older children, or to those with trauma issues? Praying with them for discernment can be helpfully framed around discovering together what situation is best for the child—the critical factor in adoptions today. Seeing the adoption process through the perspective of the child immediately deepens empathy in the potential adoptive family.

2. Connect the potentially adoptive parent(s) with resources. Deborah Siegel's concise 2015 summary of current adoption trends and updated language provides a helpful overview: http://www.socialworktoday. com/archive/111715p18.shtml. Organizations such as Send Relief (sendrelief.org), which operates a fund and counseling service for ministers and missionaries "to ignite a culture of adoption," constitute a recent development to support Christian families through the adoptive process.

3. Connect families considering adoption with families who have already adopted children. Their heart-to-heart conversations will provide space for families discerning adoption to share their hopes and fears and receive experience-rich feedback.

The writer of Ephesians uses adoption—that striking exception to the regular rules of human kinship—as the symbol of God's gracious action to include us in God's very own family. Because of God's gracious choice, we become "joint heirs with Christ" (Rom. 8:17) and "heirs of the promise" (Heb. 6:17), which grafts us onto the life-giving vine that is Jesus Christ. Like the abandoned child, we have done nothing to deserve this gracious deed, and surely without it we would have died.

God of life, who graciously adopted us into your family through Jesus Christ, grant open eyes and hearts that we might see the needs of children beyond our own family circles. Give _____ (name/s) wisdom to discern your leading in considering the adoption of a child in need of earthly parents who will make your great love known to him or her. And give us, your adopted children, the courage to redraw family lines so that we, relying on your grace, which is sufficient for the needs of all, might consider each child as our own. In the strong name of Jesus Christ I pray. Amen.

The Rev. Dr. B. Hunter Farrell
Director of the World Mission Initiative

Helpful resources for further consultation include:

> http://www.socialworktoday.com/archive/111715p18.shtml; and
>
> www.sendrelief.org.

NOTES

ANGER AND VIOLENCE

Anger and violence are among the most difficult problems for Christians to address in prayer. All of us have anger at wrongs done to us or at injustice we observe in the world. But by and large, Christian lessons on prayer do not include expressions of anger. Violence poses a similar though more complicated problem when it comes to prayer. Violence is prevalent in our world, and it appears in many forms. It appears in warfare, murder, domestic abuse, and in more subtle forms of coercion.

Non-violence, however, is a prominent part of Christian tradition, and non-retaliation is a central part of Jesus' teachings. This posture is particularly true of the New Testament's instructions on praying for enemies. Christian prayer has been shaped largely by The Lord's Prayer, which asks that God would "forgive us our debts, as we also have forgiven our debtors" (Matt. 6:12). Jesus instructed his disciples directly to "pray for those who persecute you" (Matt. 5:44), and his own example on the cross was to ask forgiveness for those who taunted and tortured him (Luke 23:34). The Apostle Paul echoes Jesus' teachings and commends this practice when he says, "Bless those who persecute you; bless and do not curse them" (Rom. 12:14), and further, "never avenge yourselves" (Rom. 12:19).

As prevalent as such teachings are, however, they are not Scripture's only perspective on anger and violence. If they were, then Christian prayer would lack vital resources to face violence and injustice. The simple injunction to forgive an enemy might alone seem encouragement to deny evil, thereby allowing it to go unchecked. It might also seem cruel to the person who suffers abuse. There is a place in Christian prayer to call for justice, to complain about present circumstances, and to petition God for the right to prevail.

The primary models for such prayer appear in the Psalms. A majority of the Psalms are prayers for help, sometimes called laments. Some of these prayers are offered by individuals who are suffering abuse or injustice or who face dire circumstances (for example, see Psalms 3, 9–10, 17, and 52). Other such prayers are uttered by communities when defeated and humiliated by enemies (see Psalms 44, 74, and 137).

The prayers for help in the Psalter may serve as examples and give language for prayer to people who are angry over some circumstance in their lives. They may also help mitigate the impulse to seek revenge on enemies.

Suggestions for reading the Psalms of Lament as model prayers include the following:

1. The prayers for help in the Psalter suggest that God is ready and willing to receive prayer expressed from the depths of the human soul (Psalm 130). Their inclusion means that God not only hears but also welcomes prayers which arise from anger and frustration.

2. The one who prays should feel free not only to express anger but also to question God's attention, or inattention, to circumstances. Jesus is the primary model in this regard. Both Matthew and Mark record Jesus' praying the opening line of Psalm 22: "My God, my God, why have you forsaken me?" (Matt. 27:46; Mark 15:34).

3. It is important to recognize, however, that the prayers for help are not petty or personal. They typically deal with life-and-death matters and are not appropriate as models for praying about small slights and disputes. These psalms express anger over the presence and power of evil in the world. They often complain of false witnesses ("Malicious witnesses rise up; they ask me about things I do not know," Ps. 35:11) or extreme injustice of a sort that many modern Western people never encounter (". . . They sit in ambush in the villages; . . . they lurk in secret like a lion in its covert; . . . they seize the poor and drag them off in their net"; see Ps. 10:7–11). Of course, some Americans do face unfair treatment (for example, in the criminal justice system), and the Psalter's prayers may apply directly to their situation. For many of us, however, an appropriate way to use these prayers as models is to practice praying on behalf of suffering and oppressed people in settings other than our own.

4. In the light of the last comment, we may read the prayers for help as pleas for God's justice, like the plea we find in The Lord's Prayer: "Your kingdom come. Your will be done, on earth as it is in heaven" (Matt. 6:10).

5. One who reads the prayers for help will frequently find petitions for God to punish or even destroy an enemy. Sometimes the language is extreme—the language of Psalm 137, for example. It is important to observe in such cases that the pray-er gives the anger to God and asks God to handle the matter, rather than the pray-er's trying to claim that place for himself or herself.

With these points as guidelines, consider praying this sample prayer alongside someone who is struggling with the issues of anger and violence:

O God, so much makes us angry, but so much of our anger is petty. We seethe when someone cuts us off in traffic. We boil inside when we learn someone has spoken ill of us. Redirect our anger toward what really matters. Help us to see the evil in the world and to direct our prayers toward those who suffer from it. Be with all the victims of abuse, those who live in places torn apart by war, and those whose lives are at risk because of disease, famine, and poverty. Let your will be done on earth as it is in heaven. In the name of Jesus we pray. Amen.

The Rev. Dr. Jerome F. D. Creach
Robert C. Holland Professor of Old Testament

Helpful resources for further consultation include:

> *The Destiny of the Righteous in the Psalms*, by Jerome F. D. Creach (Chalice, 2008);

> *A God of Vengeance? Understanding the Psalms of Divine Wrath, by Erich Zenger* (trans. Linda M. Maloney; Westminster John Knox, 1994);

> *The Message of the Psalms: A Theological Commentary*, by Walter Brueggemann (Augsburg, 1984);

> *Psalms: The Prayer Book of the Bible*, by Dietrich Bonhoeffer (Augsburg Fortress, 1974); and

> *Violence in Scripture. Interpretation: Resources for the Use of Scripture in the Church*, by Jerome F. D. Creach (Westminster John Knox, 2013).

NOTES

ANXIETY

Recently I have been struck with the response people give me when I ask them, "What gift or blessing do you deeply desire God to give you?" Invariably, many of them respond with yearning for a kind of faith or trust in God that gives them some deep inner peace which is also manifested outwardly in their demeanor and behavior. The prevalence of this desire speaks to the increased levels of anxiety that many are experiencing as they struggle to keep up with the demands of everyday family life, job pressures, financial challenges, and health concerns in today's divisive and rapidly changing technological, cultural, political, and religious contexts.

Anxious persons often experience restlessness, irritability, a sense of being overwhelmed most of the time, constant worrying about something, inability to focus, and sometimes increased heart rate, sweating, and difficulty breathing. Since anxiety involves physiological, cognitive, emotional, and behavioral aspects of a person's functioning, it is very difficult for an anxious individual to calm down. Many people in this state can and do call out to God for help when the anxiety waves toss them about at sea and threaten to overwhelm their little vessel (cf. Mark 4:35–41). But although they may believe Christ is with them, he seems asleep and appears as though he doesn't notice or care. Hence it is not helpful for pastors or others to say at the outset to anxious persons such things as "calm down," "stop worrying about it," or "everything's going to be okay," for such statements may increase their anxiety by pointing out their inadequacy to "control" the symptoms of their anxiety at that moment.

The same outcome may also ensue if the spiritual supporter starts by citing certain texts from Scripture, such as Jesus' statement in Matthew 6:25 and Luke 12:22, "do not worry about your life," and his statement in John 14:1, 27, "do not let your hearts be troubled." Such quotations, even if meant to encourage, may trigger a sense of doubt in God's promises or a sense of failure to trust God.

When anxiety escalates, it is helpful first to acknowledge compassionately that anxiety is a source of great suffering so the anxious person has a sense that you understand and are with him or her. Then invite the person to join you in a particular kind of prayer, called Breath Prayer. This kind of prayer is very simple and effective in calming the nervous system and creating a sense of spaciousness in the brain and heart so that, then and there, the person may be more ready to receive the efficacious word of God. I would lead such a prayer in this way:

We begin our prayer in the name of God, who gives us life at this very moment;
in the name of Jesus Christ, who embraces our wounds and restores us to wholeness;
in the name of the Holy Spirit, who breathes Christ's gift of peace in us.

(Speak in a calm and steady voice matching the breath of the person.)
I invite you now to
Take in a slow, deep breath;
Notice the breath entering your nose,
Feel the coolness touch the back of the throat,
Feel the rise in your belly, lungs, chest.
Gently, slowly exhale;
Notice your shoulders falling away from your ears,
Descending through your chest, lungs, belly.
Take in another slow deep breath;
Feel the rise in your belly, lungs, and chest as they fill with this life force we call breath,
The breath of the Living God, God's Ruah.
Slowly exhale, allowing the breath of God's life to fill every cell of your being.

(Here one could slowly read Mark 4:35–39,
"On that day, when evening had come, he said to them, 'Let us go across to the other side.' And leaving the crowd behind, they took him with them in the boat, just as he was. Other boats were with him. A great windstorm arose, and the waves beat into the boat, so that the boat was already being swamped. But he was in the stern, asleep on the cushion; and they woke him up and said to him, 'Teacher, do you not care that we are perishing?' He woke up and rebuked the wind, and said to the sea, 'Peace! Be still!' Then the wind ceased, and there was . . . calm," ending with a paraphrase of Jesus' words, *"Quiet now, be calm,"* then continue with the following:)

Take in another slow, deep breath,
Opening to receive the breath of Christ's Spirit,
Filling your chest, lungs, and heart with Christ's peace:
"Peace I leave with you; my peace I give to you" (John 14:27).
Slowly exhale, allowing Christ's peace
To fill every cell of your being.
And for this moment and beyond
There is space in your brain,
And Christ's gift of peace in your heart.

Glory be to God, whose power working in us
Can do infinitely more that we can ask or even imagine (Eph. 3:20);
All glory and praise be to you, O God. Amen.

After allowing the person to share anything he or she wishes after that guided-prayer experience, you might encourage the person to do short breath prayers throughout the day. Advise him or her to follow the rhythm of the inhale and exhale of breath—for example, on the inhale say or think, "My peace I give to you," and on the exhale, "Peace I leave with you." Such repetition reinforces the calming effect of Breath Prayer and the deeper rooting of Christ's words in one's mind and heart.

(A helpful suggestion: try leading this prayer with a friend before doing so with someone caught in the grip of anxiety.)

Dr. Martha A. Robbins
Joan Marshall Associate Professor Emerita of Pastoral Care and
Director of the Pneuma Institute

Helpful resources for further consultation include:

> *The Ignatian Adventure: Experiencing the Spiritual*
> *Exercises of St. Ignatius in Daily Life*, by Kevin O'Brien SJ
> (Loyola, 2011); and
>
> *Prayers for Every Need*, by William H. Kadel (C. D. Deans, 1966).

NOTES

Bereavement

How we pray for and with those who grieve, and how we pray when we ourselves are grieving, are of course related. Our own grief enables us to empathize with the grief of others. Perhaps this is why John tells us that at the tomb of his friend Lazarus, "Jesus wept" (John 11:35, KJV). How, after all, could Scripture claim that Jesus "in every respect has been tested as we are, yet without sin" (Heb. 4:15), if our common human experience of grief was unknown to him? Why else would Isaiah's Servant of the Lord empathize with the outcast to the point of sharing their sufferings (Isa. 50:4–6), to the point that the Servant could be called "a man of sorrows, and acquainted with grief" (Isa. 53:3, KJV)? So, too, we do no one any favors if in our prayers with and for the bereaved we pretend to an "elevated" spirituality in which grief has no place.

I vividly remember a courageous student who observed in a chapel sermon, "This is a very hard place to be if you are sad." In our worshiping communities, people who are hurting or depressed are likely to be left alone. We avoid them out of helplessness rather than callousness, to be sure, because we do not know what to do or say, but the end is the same— those in grief are abandoned by us. Worse, people in grief may be *jollied* by us—told to cheer up and trust in Jesus, as though their sorrow and pain were somehow a denial of their faith. As Donald Gowan ruefully observes in *The Triumph of Faith in Habakkuk*,

> Christian worship tends to be all triumph, all good
> news (even the confession of sin is not a very awesome
> experience because we know the assurance of pardon
> is coming; it's printed in the bulletin). And what does
> that say to those who, at the moment, know nothing of
> triumph?[11]

The book of Psalms is called *Tehillim*, Hebrew for "Praises," yet it contains more laments—cries for help out of pain and loss—than any other type of poem.[12] Clearly, then, frank recognition of pain and loss plays a key role in biblical worship and prayer. As Walter Brueggemann writes in his article "The Costly Lament," the loss of lament means "the loss of *genuine covenant interaction* because the second party to the covenant (the petitioner) has become voiceless or has a voice that is permitted to

---

[11] Donald E. Gowan, *The Triumph of Faith in Habakkuk* (John Knox, 1976), 38.
[12] James Luther Mays, *Psalms* (Interpretation; John Knox, 1994), 21.

speak only praise and doxology."[13] By stifling lament in our worship—and in our own prayer life—we shut off the honest engagement that a living relationship with God presumes.

So, on the one hand, our prayers must always acknowledge our common grief and pain, never deny them. But on the other hand, we must be careful not to confuse our own grief with that of others. What helped *me* in *my* pain may be of no help at all to *you* in *your* pain. So we must begin—and perhaps, end—by *listening*. There is great wisdom in the initial response of Job's friends to his anguish and loss: "They sat with him on the ground seven days and seven nights, and no one spoke a word to him, for they saw that his suffering was very great" (Job 2:13). Indeed, our presence will matter far more to those in grief than the profundity of our theology or the eloquence of our prayers. In his article "Barely Enough: Manna in the Wilderness of Depression," Frederick Niedner describes with simple eloquence the power of being present with those who are suffering:

> In the empty wilderness of someone else's darkness we
> have no cures or magic. By grace, however, we may be like
> the manna on the desert floor. God makes of our simple,
> steady acts of accompaniment a measure of "enough."
> Not much to look at, perhaps, and difficult to describe. But
> for today, enough.[14]

In that spirit, below is a simple prayer that may be comforting to pray with a person experiencing bereavement:

Lord Jesus, you wept at the tomb of your friend Lazarus. You know our loss and pain from the inside. Be with your child _____ (name) right now, we pray. Surround her/him with your love, undergird her/him with your peace and strength. Be very real to _____ (name) in these days of grief, Abba, and grant that as she/he is able to hear it, the good news of Christ's resurrection would fill her/him with hope. We pray in the name the One who has "borne our griefs, and carried our sorrows." Amen.

The Rev. Dr. Steven S. Tuell
James A. Kelso Professor of Hebrew and Old Testament

---

[13] Walter Brueggemann, "The Costly Lament," *Journal for the Study of the Old Testament* 36 (1986): 60.
[14] Frederick Niedner, "Barely Enough: Manna in the Wilderness of Depression," *Christian Century* Jan. 25 (2012): 11–13.

Helpful resources for further consultation include:

> *A Grief Observed*, by C. S. Lewis (Seabury, 1961); and

> "Services of Death and Resurrection," pages 139–71 in *The United Methodist Book of Worship* (The United Methodist Publishing House, 1992)—an excellent resource for prayers, Scriptures, and hymns for times of bereavement.

NOTES

CONFLICT AND CONTROL

Conflict is a completely normal part of human relationships and communities. Because we are all unique individuals, representing different backgrounds, beliefs, and personalities, we will often have needs, desires, or goals that are different from the people with whom we are in relationship. These differences cannot always be easily reconciled; as a result, we may experience conflict with other people—even people for whom we care very much.

The pervasive reality of conflict in our lives, however, doesn't mean we feel comfortable with it. In fact, most people feel very uneasy around conflict, and when conflict arises in intimate relationships, such as families, or in close-knit communities, such as church congregations, it can feel especially disconcerting. It can also be hard to know how to resolve conflict, particularly when the issues at stake are very important to all involved.

All these factors make it difficult to know how to pray with or for someone who is experiencing conflict. We often do not know all the details of the conflict, and we may only have one person's perspective on what is likely a complex situation. Still, because conflict often makes people anxious, and because some conflicts involve harmful words or behaviors, individuals and communities may feel a special need for support through prayer when they are encountering such struggles.

One fruitful avenue for prayer in this situation is to pray for God's will to be done. Although we often feel strongly that our own opinions are the "right" ones, the truth is that, because we are human, our perspectives are necessarily limited. We don't always know what the right course of action is, or in what direction God may be leading us as individuals or as communities of faith. For that reason, when we find ourselves in conflict with others, it can be important for us to acknowledge that we cannot control everything. Instead, we can ask God to accomplish God's will in the situation and to guide us toward the actions we need to take to help make God's will a reality. If you are having trouble finding words for such prayer, consider using The Lord's Prayer as a starting point, since it includes the petition, "Your kingdom come, Your will be done, on earth as it is in heaven" (Matt. 6:10).

Another helpful approach to prayer in situations of conflict could be to ask God to give us compassion for those with whom we disagree. In the Sermon on the Mount, Jesus instructed his disciples to "Love your enemies and pray for those who persecute you" (Matt. 5:44). Admittedly, in cases of very intense conflict this instruction can sound like an extremely challenging task. But even if we cannot find a way to understand those with whom we are in conflict, we may find that praying for them and asking God to help us have compassion for them could begin to change the way we feel toward them. Over time, such praying could help us engage our conflicts with less defensiveness and more kindness, even if we still cannot find a way to come to agreement on every issue. In situations of conflict, it is tempting to try to change others so that they will agree with us. This temptation is, at its heart, an inclination to control. In truth, though, people can only change themselves—and praying for those with whom we are in conflict may be one way of doing so, one way of helping us relinquish our desire to control.

Finally, for families and communities of faith embroiled in conflict, praying for unity may be a fruitful avenue toward healing. It is important to note here that "unity" does not mean "sameness," and we should not be praying that others would simply come over to our point of view. Neither should prayers for unity serve as substitutes for working out our conflicts directly with others—that is, we should not expect prayer to be a "magic formula" that will suddenly dissolve all the tension in our relationships and communities. But if conflicted families and communities can find ways to pray together for unity even amid their differences, they may find new spiritual strength that can help them work on their problems together. One option would be for them to reflect together on 1 Corinthians 12, which offers a beautiful image of the Church as Christ's body, and use this passage as the basis for their prayers.

If you are asked to pray with or for persons experiencing conflict, remember that you alone cannot solve the problem for that individual, family, or faith community. What you can do, though, is offer spiritual support in the midst of a time that can feel very challenging or even hurtful. Praying for guidance, compassion, and unity may help people remember that God is with them and that God wishes to bring them to a place of healing and reconciliation.

A prayer such as the one below may bring calm to those struggling through the storms of conflict and control:

Holy God, we thank you that you have created each one of us with unique gifts and callings. When we experience tension or pain because of our differences, grant us compassion for one another. Remind us that even when we disagree, we are united in our identity as your children and in the work to which you have called us. Help us now to discern your will and to follow where you lead—together. Amen.

The Rev. Dr. Leanna K. Fuller
Associate Professor of Pastoral Care

Helpful resources for further consultation include:

> *Dignity: Its Essential Role in Resolving Conflict*, by Donna Hicks (Yale University Press, 2011);
>
> *Disunity in Christ: Uncovering the Hidden Forces that Keep us Apart*, by Christena Cleveland (InterVarsity, 2013);
>
> *Reconcile: Conflict Transformation for Ordinary Christians*, by John Paul Lederach (Herald, 2014); and
>
> The Lombard Mennonite Peace Center: https://lmpeacecenter.org/.

NOTES

CRISES

Crises. They come in all forms—crises of health . . . family . . . identity . . . finances . . . even faith. At times they are intertwined. A health crisis can lead to a family crisis and then to a crisis of faith. A financial crisis can lead to an identity crisis and then to a family crisis. A crisis of faith can lead to an identity crisis and then to a family crisis before resulting in a crisis of faith. A conglomerate of crises can weave a tapestry of turmoil.

Consider this vignette. A family has been called to the bedside of a loved one whose physical health has declined to the point at which medical professionals consider further treatment options futile because her future quality of life would be compromised. She has also lost the acumen to make good decisions for herself. To complicate matters further, the patient has never shared with any family member what her wishes might be if she were to lose her decision-making capacity. So the family must make the decision whether to continue or discontinue treatment. The patient is facing a medical crisis, and given the current state of affairs, the family is also in a state of crisis for never having imagined being in this situation— one of having to make a life-altering or life-terminating decision for their loved one.

As a medical ethics intern, I once found myself meeting with a family in this very situation—a family left to make such a difficult decision. The loved one's body was breaking down, and more treatment would only cause further harm. My supervisor at the time said to the family, "Her body is already speaking for her." Those few simple words made the difference for the family.

Despite our best efforts to care for our bodies, they will always in time follow the course of our fallen world. But in several places, the Bible reminds us just who it is that our bodies belong to: "If we live, we live to the Lord, and if we die, we die to the Lord; so then, whether we live or whether we die, we are the Lord's" (Rom. 14:8). So also go Psalm 100:3, "Know that the LORD is God. It is he that made us, and we are his; we are his people, and the sheep of his pasture," and Psalm 139:13, "For it was you who formed my inward parts; you knit me together in my mother's womb." A gentle, situation-sensitive pastoral reminder of verses such as these can bring comfort in situations of physical crisis.

In another vein, consider a man who loses his job after 25 years of employment in a company that decided to restructure. After months of searching, his attempts to find new employment continue to be unsuccessful, healthcare coverage has ended, and his unemployment benefits will soon run out. He and his wife have two teenaged children— the family is struggling to make ends meet. This brewing financial crisis is putting a strain on their familial relationships as well. The husband and father did nothing to lose his job—or ever expect to—nor did the family expect to be mired in financial trouble. A family of four who regularly attended worship and church camp, who tried to be faithful members of their congregation, could now also be embarking on a crisis of faith. "Why would this hardship happen to us? What did we do to deserve it?"

Such questions could be rumbling beneath the surface of their emotions while friends and other family members, wanting to be helpful by offering advice, are unintentionally stirring the pot of confusion as the family ponders the options for the right direction to take. In such circumstances, it is always important to recall to the crisis-sufferer the One in whom we can and should put our trust. Proverbs 3:5–6 offers this reminder: "Trust in the LORD with all your heart, and do not rely on your own insight. In all your ways acknowledge him, and he will make straight your paths." In the Psalms we also find words of comfort and guidance—for example, "The LORD is my strength and my shield; in him my heart trusts; so I am helped, and my heart exults, and with my song I give thanks to him" (Ps. 28:7); "Commit your way to the LORD; trust in him, and he will act" (Ps. 37:5); and "From the end of the earth I call to you, when my heart is faint. Lead me to the rock that is higher than I; for you are my refuge . . ." (Ps. 61:2–3a).

Crises come without invitation and at inopportune times. A crisis can wrench from its moorings the faith of even a strong believer in Christ. But the strength, courage, and patience to weather through are made possible by allowing oneself to be placed in the care of our loving Creator God. This prayer invites the crisis-sufferer to do just that:

God of mercy and God of grace, the waters of this crisis are becoming overwhelming for _____ (name), who, out of fear of only making things worse, does not trust him/herself to make the right decision at this time. We know that at every turn you are there, but the journey through seems daunting. Hold the hand of _____ (name), Lord, and walk him/ her through. May your Spirit serve as _____'s (name) compass, and may _____'s (name) current misfortune and need for your help serve to remind him/her of your trustworthy love and to remind others of your grace.

The Rev. Dr. John C. Welch '02
Vice President for Student Services and Community Engagement and Dean of Students

Helpful resources for further consultation include:

Dark Night of the Soul, by St. John of the Cross (available from multiple publishers);

From the Bottom of the Heap: The Autobiography of Black Panther Robert Hillary King, by Robert Hillary King (rev. exp. ed.; PM Press, 2012);

Ministry to the Incarcerated, by Henry G. Covert (Amazon Digital, 2014); and

The Sun Does Shine: How I Found Life and Freedom on Death Row, by Anthony Ray Hinton with Lara Love Hardin (St. Martin's, 2018).

NOTES

DEPRESSION

Christ our Intercessor is praying now for us all, and in his prayers we can offer our own, thus sharing in the Christ-like work of lifting others up before God. If your prayer list has more than a few names on it, chances are that you are lifting up someone who suffers from depression. And if you do not know depression first hand, you may wonder how to pray with and for someone who does.

It is easy to think, "Well, I will just pray that the depression disappears. Maybe if enough people pray, our prayers will make it go away." So it is good to remind ourselves that prayer is not some magical power or magician's wand. If it were a magical power, we would use it to whisk away all our fears, calm every anxiety, and drive away all the inner demons of hopelessness and despair. But deep down, we know that prayer is not a magic trick that makes things disappear.

Prayer is much more powerful than that. It does not make bad things go away—it brings God close, even when our lives are full of bad things. It helps make God visible in our lives, even when the clouds within hide God from our view.

Prayer is also powerful because it brings the one who prays—you, in this case—close to the one with and for whom you pray. It connects you at the deepest possible level. Even so, if you have never suffered from depression, you may have trouble truly understanding it. But do not let that be an obstacle to praying for a friend who is depressed. Through the extraordinary spiritual power of prayer, you enter empathetically into the heart and mind of one who suffers, thus feeling what it is like to be that person at the very core of your own being. To pray for another is to enter, insofar as it is humanly possible, into what it is like to be him or her. When you pray for someone, over time you begin to understand that person better.

Christ intercedes for us because he first became one of us. In Hebrews 4:15 we read: "For we do not have a high priest who is unable to sympathize with our weaknesses, but we have one who in every respect has been tested as we are, yet without sin." Knowing that Christ our Intercessor understands the full gamut of human experience from the inside, we can bring anything to God through Christ. And so the epistle continues in verse 16: "Let us therefore approach the throne of grace with boldness, so that we may receive mercy and find grace to help in time of need."

And so we approach and boldly speak to God about the depression that is so much a part of the life of our friend. How do we describe it? Usually we speak in metaphors. Depression is darkness, we say, not a darkness that surrounds us but one that is in us, thus darkening everything else from the inside out. It is not the calm darkness that evening brings, or the startling darkness of lights going out in a storm, but a deep and paralyzing darkness brooding within, a darkness without dawn, the kind that no external light can brighten. We speak of depression as dryness, or sometimes as emptiness within. "I feel immobilized, suspended in time while everyone else goes on with life," a friend explains. Others describe it as being lost in a mist, unable to move because they cannot see themselves entering safely into the next moment or the next day. And perhaps the most common metaphor is the simple but frightening word "down." It is as though the self cannot arise within and summon up its own energy. It is down, under water, under a weight that will not go away.

Never should we think that depression brings any sort of spiritual advantage—yet the defining truth of our faith is that God meets us at the extremes. If it is possible to be too rich to enter the kingdom, perhaps it is also possible to be too happy, if by happy we mean the silly optimism so many endorse today. Where is the thirst that makes us pant for God? Where is the emptiness that opens an aching space within—a space that only God can fill? When do we feel the immobility known by the one who waited a lifetime by the pool for angels to create healing ripples in the water, and so met Jesus? When is the darkness so dark that it becomes luminous, full of an awesome glory under the sign of its opposite? Those who suffer from depression know about these things.

One popular Taizé chant begins, "Within our darkest night, you kindle the fire that never dies away, that never dies away." Joining in the endless prayer of our risen Savior, pray patiently with and for those who know the darkest night. You might consider using the prayer below in walking alongside a person suffering from depression:

Holy God, who in Jesus Christ comes into our world to be the Light that no darkness can overcome, I pray now in this moment for my friend, _____ (name). You alone know the inner mysteries of our human minds, so often filled with negative thoughts and unrelenting anxiety. Through the healing power of our Savior, Jesus Christ, grant _____ (name) relief from depression and all despair. Give _____ (name) that peace that passes all understanding, through Christ I pray. Amen.

The Rev. Dr. Ron S. Cole-Turner
H. Parker Sharp Professor of Theology and Ethics

Helpful resources for further consultation include:

Companions On The Inner Way: The Art of Spiritual Guidance, by Morton T. Kelsey (Crossroad, 1995);

Dark Night of the Soul, by St. John of the Cross (available from multiple publishers);

A Mood Apart: Depression, Mania, and Other Afflictions of the Self, by Peter C. Whybrow (Basic Books, 2015);

The Noonday Demon: An Atlas of Depression, by Andrew Solomon (Scribner, 2015); and

Undoing Depression: What Therapy Doesn't Teach You and Medication Can't Give You, by Richard O'Connor (Little, Brown and Company, 2010).

NOTES

Disability and Physical Trauma

Christian pastors and laypeople are called to pray in a thoughtful, spiritually-grounded, and non-anxious manner with all persons, including those who have physical, learning, or mental health-related disabilities and those who have experienced physical trauma. Yet praying in such a pastorally present way can be complicated for three major reasons: First, persons with disabilities and/or the experience of physical trauma respond to their embodied lives in a variety of ways, thus requiring our attention to the particular nature of each person's experience. Second, the biblical witness can lead Christians to a wide range of theological interpretations of disabilities that can manifest in disparate ways of and words used in praying. Third, personal, societal, and political assumptions often shape and are shaped by ministers' ideas about and reactions to persons with disabilities and physical traumas; those reactions affect our ways of praying and the contents of our prayers. To pray well with and for persons with disabilities or with experiences of physical trauma, we must become more deeply aware of the influences that complicate both our understandings and responses so that we can be truly present for each person in her or his wholeness before God.

First, the life experiences of persons with disabilities or with physically traumatic experiences are not uniform. Some persons may experience pain and hindrance, physical or otherwise; others may not. Some persons may feel ugly, broken, or sinful, and some may believe they are a burden on family, friends, and community; others may not—they may embrace their embodied and/or other limitations with equanimity and a sense of wholeness. Some may believe God's grace is working in their lives; others may not. Through prayer that takes into account this individual particularity without judgment, each person's life experience may be witnessed and honored as whole and true in its own manner, held by the love of God. Praying with and for those with disabilities or physical trauma best unfolds through relationships that attend to the uniqueness of each person's embodied experience.

Second, variations in the Bible's witness regarding disability have led to a range of interpretations in the church. Examples of the diversity of biblical depictions may be found in both the Old and New Testaments and can lead to different sorts of prayers. According to Genesis 1, human beings are wonderfully made in the image of God, a concept known to theologians as the *imago Dei* and witnessed in prayer by appeals to that God-like goodness in all of us. In contrast to this broad statement about human wholeness in Genesis, we find other understandings of disability grounded in portrayals of physical limitation, sickness, and affliction linked to sin, such as in the Holiness Code of the Deuteronomic history. In Deuteronomy 28, for example, God curses people's disobedience by giving them numerous diseases, madness, blindness, and various other maladies. Prayers arising from this perspective might ask God to remove the sin from a person's life through the healing of a disability. At other times in the Old Testament, however, disability appears in a more complex and slightly positive light, as with the case of Mephibosheth, the disabled grandson of King Saul who, in 2 Samuel, requires a caretaker and some level of help from others, but who also demonstrates agency of his own and is valued by King David. Prayers rooted in this sort of scriptural story might reflect this more complicated understanding of disabilities. Our interpretations of these biblical narratives often shape these and other very different approaches to prayer.

In the New Testament as well, we find an array of understandings of disability that can lead to disparities in prayers with and for persons with disabilities and/or physical trauma. In Luke 13, for example, Jesus heals a disabled woman on the Sabbath, thus causing her to praise God after her 18 years of suffering. In this case, disability is both a state from which a person desires release and a situation in which Jesus heals and liberates the person. Thus, in prayer, some people reflect the idea that disability is something that can and should be spiritually overcome. Yet Acts 9 depicts Paul's conversion through his blindness on the road to Damascus, and the loss of sight is linked in the narrative to his belief in Jesus. The Apostle then continued to have eye or other problems after that experience, as he describes in Galatians 4; and he may have to have had a scribe write down at least some of his letters due to his lack of sight, as indicated by the mention of his amanuensis, Tertius, in Romans 16. None of Paul's vision problems seem to indicate his need for spiritual healing and, in fact, they may have had a positive effect on his faith. These stories about Paul's experience might influence people's prayers regarding disability and physical trauma in a way that Luke's story might not.

The Bible's disparate depictions of persons with disabilities and physical traumas—and the variety of responses to these persons within the biblical narrative—inform Christian pastors and laypeople in diverse ways when we pray, since often these biblical stories connect with our underlying biases. So our opportunities for prayer are also opportunities to examine our assumptions about and responses to disability and to persons living with disability and physical trauma. Sometimes our biases are rooted in a tendency to define such persons by their medical conditions, mental health issues, or social or learning difficulties. Doing so can lead us to compare a person's physical, psychological, or intellectual status with what we consider a "normal" body, brain, social-emotional behavior, or personality. At times we may speculate whether a disability is congenital or has been acquired later in life in a traumatic manner as we try to determine what the difference may mean for our pastoral relationship with the person. At other times we wonder whether a person's disability is static or progressive, or we ask whether a disability only affects persons in certain groups based on age or some other status. We may inquire about what kinds of physical trauma result in particular sorts of disabilities. And, in these cases, we may be led to make decisions about how and what to pray based on the answers to these questions rather than on our relationship with the person in front of us.

Third, personal, societal, and political suppositions often shape and are shaped by ministers' ideas about and reactions to persons with disabilities and physical traumas. To pray well in this larger context, we must develop self-awareness about our biases to clear the way for the best pastoral relationships through prayer. Reflection about our personal definitions, attitudes, and practices can lead us toward a deep mindfulness that has the potential to shift our assumptions regarding disability and physical trauma and allow us to have more robust relationships with persons with disabilities or physically traumatic experiences. We might ask ourselves questions such as:

1. What *are* disability and physical trauma?

2. What is "normal" ability?

3. Who defines these categories, and *how* are they defined?

4. Does disability have to do with deficiency or abnormality in relation to bodies, brains, and personalities?

5. How is disability different from physical injury resulting in trauma?

6. What do I think about disabilities and physical traumas?

7. How do I respond currently, and how might I respond differently in the future, to persons with disabilities or persons who have survived physical trauma?

8. Why do I respond the way that I do?

9. Should my response to these people be any different from my response to anyone else?

10. Is there some way in which all of us are disabled, given that each person has unique limitations as well as gifts?

Beyond this initial personal inquiry, it is important for us to remember that disability and physical trauma also suggest something significant about the worth we and our communities assign to persons with disabilities or physical traumas. The ways we and our communities value and devalue persons is linked to how we understand human vulnerabilities and powerlessness. With our communities, we might investigate our own biases about value and vulnerability by asking ourselves these kinds of questions:

1. What are my (and our) assumptions about the nature of human vulnerability?

2. Do I (and we) see people with obvious physical or mental vulnerabilities as less valuable than those who have less obvious vulnerabilities?

3. In what ways do I (and we) dehumanize others through categorization and labeling?

4. In what ways do I (and we) uphold the value and worth of persons with disabilities?

We might consider the manner in which we, along with others in our communities, reject or exclude others whom we deem lesser persons than ourselves, for our tendency to value some people more than others shapes the ways we pray as individuals and as communities.

These considerations about value and vulnerability connect with political realities that both form and are formed by our approaches to prayer. Policies and practice at every level of government influence and are influenced by our assumptions about disability and physical trauma. In the United States, we have experienced wildly divergent socio-political reactions to those whom we have deemed disabled. Some of these reactions have resulted in dehumanization and exclusion (whether intended or not) of persons with disabilities and physical traumas, while others have resulted in inclusion and the recognition of agency in such persons. For example, our city, state, and federal governments have sometimes housed persons with disabilities in mental health or medical institutions, far away from the workings of society; at other times, our government has diligently worked to incorporate persons with disabilities into our homes, educational institutions, the work force, public transportation, cultural events, and churches and other religious institutions. These public reactions mold and are molded by our private assumptions and reactions, thus affecting the life of prayer with and for persons with disabilities and physical traumas.

As we investigate and sort through our views of disability and physical trauma and our responses to both, we can begin to find new spaces for and ways of praying with such persons. In the Christian community, the questions engendered by individual, communal, and political understandings of disability and physical trauma must be accompanied by foundational theological considerations linked to the Bible and our Christian traditions. As we consider praying, we might ask ourselves about what it means to be fully human and whole. We might wonder what Genesis is suggesting when it says human beings—all of us—are made in the image of God. It is pastorally appropriate to determine whether we think disability has something (or nothing) to do with sin, purity, and/or grace. We might investigate whether we believe God can be a good God when a person suffers a damaging traumatic event or lives a whole life with a disability.

Whatever our answers to these inquiries, we can be sure that effective prayer with and for persons living with disability and physical trauma usually avoids reinforcing the unexamined assumption that all such persons feel or experience the same thing. Effective prayer also comes from a place of clarity about the minister's understanding of the biblical witnesses regarding disability and physical trauma. Effective prayer does not rely solely upon social and political definitions of human value and worth—it is also and importantly rooted in sound theological reflection. Pastorally, our prayers need to take into account the uniqueness of each person before God. They need to witness that a person with disabilities is not defined first and only by what she or he may appear to us to be lacking, but also and importantly by her or his God-given gifts. Pastoral presence in this situation calls us to release our own and society's ideas about disability and physical trauma and to learn from and with such persons about their own rich experiences and about God by offering our friendship, love, and communion. In praying with and for them, ministers must recognize disabled and physically traumatized people as whole persons and walk with them down the paths on which they find themselves in their spiritual journeys as children of a loving God. Consider using these and similar prayers in such ministry; the first prayer here is attributed to St. Teresa of Ávila:

Christ has no body now but yours. No hands, no feet on earth but yours. Yours are the eyes through which he looks compassion on this world. Yours are the feet with which he walks to do good. Yours are the hands through which he blesses all the world. Yours are the hands, yours are the feet, yours are the eyes, you are his body. Christ has no body now on earth but yours.

— St. Teresa of Ávila

Loving Creator God, you have made each person in your image, and you invite each person to live in wholeness through relationship with you. Be with us in our doubts and limitations, our gifts and strengths. Heal every one of us from the false assumptions about ourselves and others that divide us, so that we may be unified with each other in our love for you. Amen.

Dr. Mary O'Shan Overton
Director of the Center for Writing and Learning Support

Helpful resources for further consultation include:

Becoming Friends of Time: Disability, Timefullness, and Gentle Discipleship, by John Swinton (Baylor University Press, 2018);

Becoming Human, by Jean Vanier (2nd ed.; Paulist, 2008);

The Bible, Disability, and The Church: A New Vision of the People of God, by Amos Yong (Eerdmans, 2011);

The Disabled God: Toward a Liberatory Theology of Disability, by Nancy Eisland (Abingdon, 1994);

Madness: American Protestant Responses to Mental Illness, by Heather H. Vacek (Baylor University Press, 2015); and

Theology and Down Syndrome: Reimagining Disability in Late Modernity, by Amos Yong (Baylor University Press, 2007).

NOTES

DISCERNMENT

Two roads diverged in a yellow wood, and sorry I could not travel both and be one traveler, long I stood (Robert Frost, "The Road Not Taken").

For to me, living is Christ and dying is gain. If I am to live in the flesh, that means fruitful labor for me; and I do not know which I prefer (Phil. 1:21–22).

"Pastor, for my next job I've got to choose between A, B, and C (job, house, school for my child, etc.)—can you help me decide what is best?" Or "Pastor, can I meet with you to discuss what God wants me to do about XYZ situation?" Such requests are calls for discernment, for helping someone or a group of people—or perhaps even your own self—find the guidance or direction needed to make a godly choice. Even people who generally have a less-than-robust prayer life are willing to talk with God when faced with a difficult or weighty decision. Sometimes they choose to seek advice from someone they view as God's representative—a minister, church-going relative, or wise and trusted friend. The process becomes discernment when it includes conversations (prayer) with God and others in order to seek God's will and perspective on the situation at hand.

Several years ago a friend recommended *In Search of Guidance*, by Dallas Willard—the first book I read on the topic of discernment. A revised edition was published under its current title, *Hearing God: Developing a Conversational Relationship with God*, which highlights the importance of both conversation and relationship in seeking discernment. It's a book that I still treasure, re-read from time to time, and frequently recommend to others. This book helped me understand that God wants us to know God's will for our lives and that God isn't interested in playing hide-and-seek games with us or waiting till we've reached some high level of spiritual attainment near sainthood to let us in on divine direction. Similarly in a sense to our experiences with healthy and life-giving human relationships, God desires that as we grow in relationship with Christ, we become mature people who naturally perceive and desire what would be pleasing and glorifying to God in our actions, attitudes, and choices. As we grow in our knowledge and love of God, we become better discerners.

In the preface to his book, Willard describes a picture of his children happily playing in the yard. He writes that he had no preference for the particular sort of play they might undertake. As long as his kids were engaged in any of a number of acceptable options, they were completely within their father's will. Willard then comments, "Generally speaking we are in God's will whenever we are leading the kind of life he wants for us. And that leaves a lot of room for initiative on our part, which is essential: our individual initiatives are central to his will for us."[15]

I have repeatedly found this comment helpful because there are times when we struggle to come to a definitive answer or the one, correct (and, often implied, perfect) decision or choice, when God may, in fact, not have a preference for a specific option among a group of equally good possibilities. There may be two or more good choices. Practically speaking, each of these possibilities offers us a different path with varying circumstances, blessings, and challenges that will present unique opportunities for nurturing our relationship with God and helping us mature spiritually. For example, choosing one job or house over the other acceptable options may open a door to a particular set of people and circumstances that will provide opportunities for us to grow in patience and generosity. Choosing another equally good job or house may lead to a different door or path to grow in these same virtues—or perhaps other virtues entirely.

God's concern is that our choices continue to allow for growth in our relationship with God (knowing and loving God more deeply, fully, and experientially) and in our character's growing resemblance to the character of Jesus, were he to be living life's path in our shoes. When others come to us seeking our help for discernment, we need to emphasize the importance of taking into account how each option might affect their relationship with God and opportunities for spiritual growth at least as much as considering the other, more easily perceived pros and cons that modern folks tend to include in our decision-making processes.

Another book I've found very helpful toward understanding discernment is *Weeds Among the Wheat, Discernment: Where Prayer and Action Meet*, by Thomas Green, S.J., a noted Ignatian spiritual director and retreat leader. This book developed from a series of lectures and classes on discernment he taught to clergy, religious, and committed lay people on how to apply the "rules" developed in St. Ignatius of Loyola's Spiritual Exercises to the issues of discernment that arise in the lives of all believers. Green describes discernment as an art and a gift—an art because "it is learned by doing, by trial and error. And it is a gift, not primarily the fruit of personal effort, but God's gift to those who love and are loved by him."[16]

---

[15] Dallas Willard, *Hearing God* (InterVarsity, 1999), 11.
[16] Thomas Green, *Weeds Among the Wheat* (Ave Maria, 1984), 22.

Both Willard and Green write about learning to distinguish between God's voice/direction and that of the conflicting false voices/direction of "the world, the flesh, and the devil," which make seeking after discernment necessary and, at times, difficult. Willard approaches the topic from a more evangelical, biblical direction, and his chapter "The Still Small Voice and Its Rivals" offers practical, grounded, and accessible teaching on recognizing the variety of ways in which God speaks. Green covers similar ground from an Ignatian perspective by concentrating more on the experiences of desolation and consolation that come from God's work in our lives. Both books are helpful for a Christian leader's formation and library.

And now some practical remarks about discernment. Over the years, I've learned to hear God's voice in ways that generally remain consistent to my experience and relationship with God. I pay more notice when God catches my attention or communicates with me in ways that have been significant to my relationship with Christ. On the one hand, I've had experiences in which I knew unmistakably that God had spoken or nudged me, thus making God's will and perspective known—almost always when I hadn't been actively seeking to hear from God. Conversely, at other times, no matter how hard I've tried or prayed, I haven't been able to make God speak or force God's will to be made explicitly known to me. Rarely does God let me know what's going to happen in the future. When God does so, the disclosure may have the purpose of making me better able and prepared to serve others. Hearing from God and not hearing from God both tend to grow me in humility, strengthen my trust in God's providence, and build up my faith.

Further, at various times God has given me guidance or knowledge that I have no idea how to apply—because the time to use it will come later. After making sincere but failed attempts to understand such revelations, I've learned to put them aside, continue walking my current path, and wait patiently for God's further direction when the time is right. All such experiences are part of the great adventure of walking with God through one's own life and in ministry alongside others.

This prayer of St. Richard of Chichester can be helpful to those struggling to discern God's direction and will:

Thanks be to you, my Lord Jesus Christ, for all the benefits you have given me, for all the pains and insults you have borne for me. O most merciful redeemer, friend and brother, may I know you more clearly, love you more dearly, and follow you more nearly, day by day. Amen.

Consider also this prayer of Thomas Merton:

My Lord God, I have no idea where I am going. I do not see the road ahead of me. I cannot know for certain where it will end. Nor do I really know myself, and the fact that I think that I am following your will does not mean that I am actually doing so. But I believe that the desire to please you does in fact please you. And I hope I have that desire in all that I am doing. I hope that I will never do anything apart from that desire. And I know that if I do this you will lead me by the right road, though I may know nothing about it. Therefore will I trust you always, though I may seem to be lost and in the shadow of death. I will not fear, for you are ever with me, and you will never leave me to face my perils alone.[17]

The Rev. Dr. Catherine M. Brall
Director of Field Education

Helpful resources for further consultation include:

> *Hearing God: Developing a Conversational Relationship with God*, by Dallas Willard (InterVarsity, 1999);
>
> *Thoughts in Solitude*, by Thomas Merton (Farrar, Straus and Giroux, 1999); and
>
> *Weeds Among the Wheat, Discernment: Where Prayer and Action Meet*, by Thomas Green (Ave Maria, 1984).

---

[17] Thomas Merton, *Thoughts in Solitude* (Farrar, Straus and Giroux, 1999), 79.

NOTES

Discouragement

"Do not fear, for I am with you, do not be afraid, for I am your God; I will strengthen you, I will help you, I will uphold you with my victorious right hand" (Isa. 41:10). Discouragement is a feeling that everyone experiences from time to time. Sometimes it may last for an hour, sometimes a day. Sometimes it lasts for weeks, and at other times it is a season of life. Everyone who feels discouraged has a personal experience that cannot be compared to that of another. Yet, whether it lasts for an hour or a much longer period, discouragement is an emotion that needs to be handled with empathy, caring, and prayer. If you are the one praying with or for someone who is discouraged, here are a few suggestions for reflection.

Discouragement comes in many different forms. It comes to the person who is dealing with a crumbling marriage and is unemployed; the person who is recovering from cancer only to find out that the cancer has recurred; the person who has helped a child go through the recovery process from drug abuse only to find out that the child is using again; the person who is adjusting to the loss of a loved one; or the pastor who is in the midst of controversy in the church to which he/she has been called.

Discouragement is no respecter of persons. When people find life weighing them down, they are in need of conversation and prayer. So allow the person who is discouraged a chance to talk about the current circumstances. Being heard and knowing that someone is actively listening is of vital importance. Be an active listener! Make certain that you understand the difficulty and, in conversation, paraphrase your understanding of the problem back to the person to whom you're listening. Refrain from offering solutions and judgment. Solving the issue is not your role. Don't listen to respond—listen to hear.

When engaging in active listening, it is possible to pray for the actual concerns of the discouraged person. Lift them up to God by name and circumstance. True, God already knows each of our needs, but prayer makes a difference. What is so important about prayer? In prayer we are praising, thanking, and glorifying God. Certainly, we can also pray for different circumstances! Most of all we are praying for change. We are not asking *God* to change—we are asking God to change *us*. Through prayer our attitudes, thoughts, and reactions to the situations in our life are changed. God changes our hearts through prayer.

In his book *Mere Christianity*, C. S. Lewis writes:

> Imagine yourself as a living house. God comes in to rebuild
> that house. At first, perhaps, you can understand what
> He is doing. He is getting the drains right and stopping
> the leaks in the roof and so on; you knew that those jobs
> needed doing and so you are not surprised. But presently
> He starts knocking the house about in a way that hurts
> abominably and does not seem to make any sense. What
> on earth is He up to? The explanation is that He is building
> quite a different house from the one you thought of—
> throwing out a new wing here, putting on an extra floor
> there, running up towers, making courtyards. You thought
> you were being made into a decent little cottage: but
> He is building a palace. He intends to come and live in it
> Himself.[18]

Help the discouraged person invite Jesus to indwell him or her. It is God's plan to live in our hearts. In *Prayer: Finding the Heart's True Home*, Richard Foster talks about prayer as a means of being refreshed. Through prayer we learn to throw our arms up into the air and fall back into the ever-loving arms of God while trusting that God will renew us day by day.[19] In *Disappointment with God*, Philip Yancey writes and elaborates the statement, "The alternative to disappointment with God seems to be disappointment without God."[20] These books are good resources for facing the issue of discouragement.

The uncertainty in all of life requires a resilient faith and total trust in the one true God, who sees the beautiful tapestry of our entire life, not just the messy spot where we are currently living. Encouraging a person's trust that God is faithful in all things can be a tremendous source of strength to the one who's discouraged. Many passages of Scripture that relate to the topic of discouragement are helpful in nurturing such trust in God. Consider these two from 2 Corinthians: "We are afflicted in every way, but not crushed; perplexed, but not driven to despair; persecuted but not forsaken; struck down, but not destroyed" (4:8–9); and ". . . for we walk by faith, not by sight" (5:7). See also these verses:

---

[18] C. S. Lewis, *Mere Christianity* (MacMillan Co., 1960), 160.
[19] Richard J. Foster, *Prayer: Finding the Heart's True Home* (HarperCollins, 1992).
[20] Philip Yancey, *Disappointment with God* (Zondervan, 1997), chap. 30.

When the righteous cry for help, the LORD hears, and rescues them from all their troubles. The LORD is near to the brokenhearted, and saves the crushed in spirit. Many are the afflictions of the righteous, but the LORD rescues them from them all (Ps. 34:17–19).

He heals the brokenhearted, and binds up their wounds (Ps. 147:3).

Cast your burden on the LORD, and he will sustain you; he will never permit the righteous to be moved (Ps. 55:22).

Bless the LORD, O my soul, and do not forget all his benefits (Ps. 103:2).

Those who wait for the LORD shall renew their strength, they shall mount up with wings like eagles, they shall run and not be weary, they shall walk and not faint (Isa. 40:31).

I will lead the blind by a road they do not know, by paths they have not known I will guide them. I will turn the darkness before them into light, the rough places into level ground. These are the things I will do, and I will not forsake them (Isa. 42:16).

For surely I know the plans I have for you, says the LORD, plans for your welfare and not for harm, to give you a future with hope (Jer. 29:11).

Come to me, all you that are weary and are carrying heavy burdens, and I will give you rest (Matt. 11:28).

My God will fully satisfy every need of yours according to his riches in glory in Christ Jesus (Phil. 4:19).

A helpful resource of 10 prayers to address discouragement can be found at http://www.beliefnet.com/ilovejesus/features/10-prayers-to-fight-discouragement.aspx?p=2. One such prayer, based on Hebrews 4:10, reads:

Oh Heavenly Father, though I am dealing with disappointment and obstacles, I rest in the fact that You are still on the throne. Lead me to enter into Your rest O Lord and not be disillusioned by the current circumstances;

through Jesus Christ your benevolent Son our Lord, who lives and reigns with You and the Holy Spirit, in Oneness and power, now and forever. Amen.

As well, consider personalizing the following prayer in praying with a person struggling through discouragement:

Holy and most loving God, you know our every need, our every hurt, and our every pain. In times when we feel discouraged by the circumstances of life, provide us with strength, guidance, and wisdom. Remind us that you did not call us to be successful but to be faithful and trusting. I pray for my brother/sister _____ (name) and ask that, as he/she deals with _____ (difficulty), he/she is filled with the power of the Holy Spirit and knows the peace that comes only through being a beloved child of God. When words fail _____ (name), give him/her your words that the light of Christ may overcome the darkness and joy fill his/her heart. In the name of our risen and living Lord, Jesus the Christ, I pray. Amen.

The Rev. Carolyn E. Cranston '99
Director of Alumnae/i and Church Relations

Helpful resources for further consultation include:

> *Disappointment with God*, by Philip Yancey (Zondervan, 1997), chap. 30;
>
> *Mere Christianity*, by C. S. Lewis (MacMillan Co., 1960); and
>
> *Prayer: Finding the Heart's True Home*, by Richard J. Foster (HarperCollins, 1992).

NOTES

Doubt and Uncertainty About Faith

Trying to pray as, for, or with someone in the grips of uncertainty or lack of faith is a little like a modern poet's trying to compose a new piece in the "genteel lyricism" of the 19th-century masters. Jewish poet Joy Ladin has written about how much of modern poetic expression is a skeptical reaction to the tendency of earlier poets to speak in universalizing terms about our world with a perspective "from above," as it were.

The counter-reaction has produced what Allen Ginsburg called "the aesthetics of relative truth," whereby poets express "from below" individual perspectives, voices, and biographical anecdotes, while leaving unanswered—or even ridiculing—the larger question of truth. Entering the genre of prayer, especially as enshrined in our liturgies and collective Christian praxis, can ask skeptics to speak suddenly with a feigned surety, or at least with a voice that to their minds ignores deep doubts and uncertainties. How do we pray to God when it is in fact God, God's character, or God's involvement in the world that is the very thing in question?

We need to recognize at the outset that that question can stem from different places in the mind and heart. For some people, fleeting waves or prolonged states of doubt and uncertainty are primarily intellectual in nature and stem from encountering challenging perspectives in the classroom, in various forms of media, or in other persons. Such is common on college campuses today, as religious students increasingly find themselves ill equipped to respond to new viewpoints they perceive as contrary to their faith. At the other end of the spectrum, uncertainty and doubt may arise as one responds to difficult experiences in life—especially suffering, tragedy, and disappointment—that force a person to rethink his or her cherished theological convictions.

In both the intellectual and the experiential realms—and all cases in between—it is important to remember that the words we choose to speak will not always be understood in the way we intend. So even when our prayers and words of advice are theologically sound and intellectually rich, and even when our encouragement stems from genuine good will, our words can still communicate an underlying impatience with another's doubt and questioning. They may communicate, unhelpfully, our real hope that the difficulty will soon "end" and "things can get back to normal." I know from experience on the receiving end of such pastoral counsel that it is far more helpful—and surely more difficult—to begin with a ministry of presence and to practice a posture of listening. Our presence and our prayers should embody the truth that there is space in our tent to name difficulties honestly, and there is a language of lament to voice them.

Jesus himself embodied this truth in his last moments on the cross, and it may be particularly helpful to reflect on this episode and allow it to permeate our prayers. At the very climax of Jesus' earthly ministry, when he is doing precisely what he had set out to do, we observe in the cry of dereliction, "My God, my God, why have you forsaken me?" (Matt. 27:46), a profound encounter with doubt, uncertainty, and a sense of failure. Yet the cry of dereliction also shows that Jesus dealt with those realities at this harrowing moment by naming them and voicing them—with utter honesty—to God.

Indeed, there is a paradox here that should also characterize our prayers. Prayer at this moment is hardly a setting aside of intellectual and existential struggles to assume a confident and assertive voice "from above" that is alien to us. It is, rather, expressing that very struggle to God, just as Jesus does on the cross. Importantly, however, the expression of that struggle is directed toward God in words of desperation, as Jesus cites an opening line of a Psalm of David: "My God, my God, why have you forsaken me? Why are you so far from helping me, from the words of my groaning?" (Ps. 22:1). There is, therefore, both here and in the Psalms of Lament (also a helpful resource) in general, a whole genre of speech that invites us to ask, to question, to challenge, and to give ourselves to God in the process.[21]

It can also be helpful to remind those struggling particularly with intellectual doubts and uncertainties that the modern understanding of "faith" has been essentially to reduce it to "belief." The upshot is that, especially in a Protestant context, temporary or prolonged doubt can create tremendous anxiety. In the Bible, however—both the Old and New Testaments—faith is much better understood as a disposition of trust in God that manifests in how we live. It may be helpful here to recall in our prayers biblical scenes that define faith better than our contemporary culture is wont to do. One such scene appears at the beginning of Jesus' ministry when he calls four brothers to follow him. He does not give them a theology lesson at first and ask them to sign on; rather, he utters a call and invites them to take the risk of launching out to follow him. This following is what Jesus asks of us, too: he utters a call and invites us to respond in faith—trust manifested in life.

---

[21] Psalms of Individual Lament: 3–5; 7; 9–10; 13–14; 17; 22; 25–28; 31; 36; 39–40:12–17; 41–43; 52–57; 59; 61; 64; 70–71; 77; 86; 89; 120; 139; 141–142; Psalms of Community Lament: 12; 44; 58; 60; 74; 79–80; 83; 85; 89–90; 94; 123; 126; 129.

Faith is not having utter certainty about the things of God, nor is it knowing all the answers to life's difficult questions. Faith does not begin with understanding; rather, it "seeks understanding," as St. Anselm so wisely put it. Our prayers can be acts of seeking understanding.

One final confession: I am sometimes tempted to frame my prayers as little apologetics lessons or theodicies. But then I recall the example of Christ in Dostoevsky's *Grand Inquisitor*. How does he respond to the questioning of the priest who asserts—and sometimes with brilliant argumentation—that Christ was wrong to refuse the devil's three temptations in the desert? We assume that Jesus has his superior reasons. But offering them is not what he does in Dostoevsky's novel. His response is far more mysterious and frankly more profound: he merely kisses the priest. The gesture points to a disarming love beyond words. It is an embodied prayer. Here the fruits of the Spirit—particularly peace and patience—are near to hand. Can we strive to make our prayers with and for others, especially those struggling with uncertainty and doubt about their faith, a kiss of that nature? Consider sharing this prayer with them:

Lord, we do not know what to pray, and we do not know what to make of you. We are like Jacob on the banks of the Jabbok, on the border of the promised land, looking in from the outside. But like Jacob in that pivotal moment, we will never stop wrestling with you. We cry out to you now from the place of our estrangement. Bring us home, we pray. Amen.

Dr. Tucker S. Ferda
Visiting Assistant Professor of New Testament

Helpful resources for further consultation include:

> *Answering God: The Psalms as Tools for Prayer*, by Eugene H. Peterson (HarperOne, 1991);
>
> *Dark Night of the Soul*, by St. John of the Cross (available from multiple publishers);
>
> *Everything Starts from Prayer*, by Saint (Mother) Teresa (White Cloud, 2018);
>
> *Faith at the Edge: A Book for Doubters*, by Robert N. Wennberg (Eerdmans, 2009); and
>
> *Pensées*, by Blaise Pascal (Oxford University Press, 2008).

NOTES

Dying Without Knowing God

In the spring of 2018, Pope Francis had a quiet conversation with a worried child about his nonbelieving (and deceased) father; he turned the boy's torture into a teachable moment for all those gathered around him. Technically, he left the judgment up to God ("God is the one who says who goes to heaven"), but in effect he assured this boy that his father was in God's presence, even though in his life he "did not have the gift of faith." He emphasized the boy's insistence that his father was a "good man," the father's permission for his children to be baptized (despite his own lack of faith), and the conviction that all of us are "children of God."

I am sure many people were touched by the Pope's connection with the boy Emmanuele and his desire to set the child's mind at rest. But biblically, both the pontiff's assurance and his grounds for it are unfounded. He encouraged the children gathered around him to go beyond what Hans Von Balthasar termed the hope that all will be saved and urged them to declare that the boy's father is indeed now in God's presence. His major theological point was that all are children of God. Both moves, however, are countered by John 1:12—"But to all who received him, who believed in his name, he gave power to become children of God." We are born God's beloved creatures; we become God's children (on the basis of Christ's actions) when we turn to him.

So what should we think about people who die without knowing God? It is helpful to remember that human beings long for assurances: well-meaning Christians have vacillated between the tolerance expressed by the Pope and the plain-speaking of those who insist that only individuals who have uttered the sinner's prayer are "saved." I believe that, instead, we must acknowledge mystery. Just as no one knows when Christ will return, so we must not judge the final fate of others—either positively or negatively (1 Cor. 4:4). This reserve is particularly important in the case of people who have not made a public profession of faith in Christ. But it is not simply a reverent agnosticism to which we are called. After all, these people may not know God, but God knows them and considers them dear! And so, we are called to pray for them—and to pray in the assurance that the ones whom *we* love, God loves infinitely more. God alone perceives the trajectory upon which they have traveled and continue to move; if there is even a spark, we can be sure that "He will not . . . quench a smoldering wick" (Matt. 12:20, recalling Isa. 42:3).

Some people will respond, "What use is there to pray for those who have already died—surely the die is cast, and there is nothing more for us to do?" But where is that written in Scripture? Yes, Hebrews 9:27 tells us that "it is appointed for mortals to die once, and after that the judgment"—but this passage does not assert that nothing can happen between death and the final judgment of a person. It seems that many of us have taken this phrase beyond its meaning, perhaps in reaction to the silliness (and blasphemy) of medieval "indulgences." Have we thrown out the baby with the bathwater? We know that we cannot pay for our relatives to be saved; we know that God is the judge and that one who rejects Christ finally (and sadly) may be allowed that freedom. But why should we think that our prayers for these beloved ones must cease at their moment of death? On what grounds do we assume that there is no further growth toward God or in glory after death? No, our love demands that we do not turn off our concern like a switch, as though death had the final say. Instead, we continue to hope and pray for their movement toward a God who has conquered the power of death and who "desires everyone to be saved and to come to the knowledge of the truth" (1 Tim. 2:4).

What is happening to our loved ones after death is a mystery, but God's love for them is assured. Neither can our love for them be broken by death. Our friend or family member might not have "known" God in a self-conscious way during life—but are there not many ways of knowing? More than that, he or she was known by God, the One "who gives life to the dead and calls into existence the things that do not exist" (Rom. 4:17). Who is so great a God as our God? He is the God who does wonders—including calling us into his presence, confirming even the smallest seed of faith, and (as C. S. Lewis puts it), giving us faces so that we can see and love him.

We are neither to give blithe assurances nor grieve as people who have no hope; rather, let us cast our care upon—and direct our hope toward—the God of creation and of resurrection, who has made provision for all by taking on everything that it is to be human and by vanquishing sin and death.

O Heavenly Father, in your Son Jesus Christ you have given to us sure hope and the assurance that you hold every one of your creatures in your care. We pray that you would shed forth upon your whole Church, both in paradise and on earth, the bright beams of your light and heavenly comfort. Help us, we pray, to cast our cares upon you, in the hope that we, with those whom we love, may enter, in the last day, into your eternal glory. Give us faithfulness in prayer and the power to live as people who believe in the communion of saints, the forgiveness of sins, and the resurrection to life everlasting. By your Holy Spirit, strengthen in us this faith and hope all the days of our life, through the love of your Son, Jesus Christ our Savior, who lives and reigns with you, Father, and the Holy Spirit, one God, forever and ever. Amen.

Dr. Edith M. Humphrey
William F. Orr Professor of New Testament

Helpful resources for further consultation include:

> *Dare We Hope "That All Men Be Saved"?* by Hans Urs von Balthasar (2nd ed.; Ignatius, 2014); and

> *The Great Divorce*, by C. S. Lewis (rev. ed.; HarperOne, 2015).

NOTES

Family Problems

In the opening verses of the novel *Anna Karenina*, Leo Tolstoy writes, "All happy families are alike; each unhappy family is unhappy in its own way." Whether he is accurate about happy families is unclear; but he is right that we should be careful not to generalize about families that are struggling. For family problems emerge in many unique forms: financial stress, addiction, physical or mental illness, grief, job loss, divorce, relocation, adultery, and many, many more. And even the healthiest transitions—ushered by the birth of a child, empty-nesting, aging parents, even retirement—can be stress-inducing.

Family life is complicated. We can find comfort in recognizing that this fact has been true from the beginning of time. From the outset, the Bible is filled with examples of tension between spouses—Adam and Eve find themselves ashamed before the Lord (Gen. 3:7ff.); Abraham and Sarah lose hope for having a child (Gen. 16:1ff.). Sibling rivalries and betrayals frequently appear—Cain murders his brother Abel (Gen. 4:1ff.); Joseph's jealous brothers sell him into slavery to the Egyptians (Gen. 37:12ff.). Children clash with their parents and in-laws—Jacob colludes with his mother to fool his father in order to gain the birthright (Gen. 27:1ff.); later, Jacob is fooled by his father-in-law into marrying Leah instead of Rachel (Gen. 30:21ff.). The situation does not magically improve in the new "household of God" instituted by Jesus; we see the same tensions, rivalries, and clashes among the "brothers and sisters" of Christ in his Church.

What can we do? First, it helps to acknowledge that family life has never been easy . . . though it is easy to despair or place blame. The truth is that all households struggle. We are tempted to see only joy and success in other people's homes, but the proverbial warning, "Never compare your insides to other people's outsides," is spot on. We have no idea what struggles people endure behind closed doors.

Second, it helps to identify the particular struggles a family is experiencing rather than generalize. As people who come alongside individuals and families in their struggles, it is above our "pay grade" to offer diagnoses, but it can be reassuring to help them name their pain. It might be the feeling of having failed their children by divorcing, losing a mortgage, or not parenting well. It might be dread from no longer knowing what or whom to trust after being cheated on by one's spouse or the relapsing of one's parent into alcohol abuse. It might be the sense of isolation that comes when members of a family are fighting with each other. It might be a perfect storm of a spouse's job loss, a child's diagnosis, and an aging parent's illness. Even when multiple stressors combine, naming the particular feelings and issues helps make a person or family feel slightly less global and cataclysmic about the struggles faced.

Third, it is crucial that people recognize they are not alone. Encouraging people to find help—in talking with you, discovering a 12-Step program or support group, or even volunteering with others—brings comfort in distress. In times of deep conflict within a family, a counselor can be especially helpful to move toward peace and possibly reconciliation as well.

Above all, our faith reminds us that God is with us through it all: "And remember, I am with you always, to the end of the age," Jesus tells us (Matt. 28:20). Paul confirms this statement when he writes, "I am convinced that neither death, nor life, nor angels, nor rulers, nor things present, nor things to come, nor powers, nor height, nor depth, nor anything else in all creation, will be able to separate us from the love of God in Christ Jesus our Lord" (Rom. 8:38–39).

What attitude of prayer is helpful? As the Psalms remind us, there are many attitudes of prayer that are appropriate, depending on the need: lament for one's pain or grief; confession of one's own failure or complicity; pleas for healing of body or mind, and the mending of broken relationships. Over time, the particular prayer needs will likely change. But we know that placing all our fears, worries, yearning, and confession at the throne of grace never ends. And who knows? Perhaps one day a prayer of thanksgiving will be in order, too—thanksgiving for fences mended, feelings softened, relationships restored.

The following prayer uses helpful language for praying with people facing family problems:

Gracious God, you know all too well what it is like for your family to face problems. You have seen your sons and daughters struggle with deep pain, fight with one another, fail to fulfill their promises, and even walk away from you. There is no struggle that you do not know intimately, and we are grateful for your care for us.

We are bold to ask, then, Lord, for your presence with us. Forgive our own failures, and help us to forgive those who have failed us. Mend our brokenness, and heal those we love. Help us to receive the love that others offer and not to be ashamed of our need. And, above all, dearest Lord, help us to know deep in our hearts that we are not alone. All these things we pray in the name of our brother and savior, Jesus Christ. Amen.

The Rev. Dr. Christine A. Chakoian
Vice President for Seminary Advancement

Helpful resources for further consultation include:

> *Making Faithful Decisions at the End of Life*, by Nancy Duff (Westminster John Knox, 2018);
>
> *Reclaiming Conversation: The Power of Talk in a Digital Age*, by Sherry Turkle (Penguin, 2015); and
>
> *Sacred Marriage: What If God Designed Marriage to Make Us Holy More Than to Make Us Happy?* by Gary L. Thomas (Zondervan, 2015).

NOTES

Financial Distress

> Therefore do not worry, saying, "What will we eat?" or "What will we drink?" or "What will we wear?" For it is the Gentiles who strive for all these things; and indeed your heavenly Father knows that you need all these things. But strive first for the kingdom of God and his righteousness, and all these things will be given to you as well (Matt. 6:31–32).

Financial hardships are a reality in life. As companies downsize, illness strikes, resources are used unwisely, recent graduates lack job prospects, and others age without the necessary resources for financial support, personal debt can mount. Many people are facing difficult financial situations and do not know where to turn. So they come to their pastor or spiritual advisor seeking prayer and guidance. Scripture references are always a sound way to begin such conversations, but for the person seeking help, it is often difficult to believe in the heart what the head knows to be true.

When a person seeks you out to ask for help, listen. Often people in need don't come expecting a solution to the problem; they simply want to be able to tell their story without fear of judgment. Be open and affirming as you listen. Avoid the temptation to preach the prosperity gospel. I have found it to be very true that the more we give to others the more we find God providing for our needs, but we do not give to others so that God will give us what we want. We give in response to God's love and faithfulness. Prayer is the best way to connect with God and to come into God's guiding presence.

We do not pray to change God—we pray to change ourselves and how we deal with our circumstances. Prayer opens us up to hearing what God has to say to us. Sometimes the more broken we are, the easier it is to humble ourselves before God and patiently wait for guidance.

I am reminded of a wonderful story in a little book by Anthony Bloom titled *Beginning to Pray*. Bloom talks about the need to let go of everything, to give our lives and trust to God totally. He wrote about going somewhere with a friend as a teenager and planning to arrive at a time when they would surely be offered lunch. Due to a train delay, they arrived after the lunch hour and felt extremely hungry. They asked whether they could be given something to eat. The only food available was half a cucumber. Bloom couldn't imagine being grateful to receive his share—a quarter of a cucumber!—but his friend, a strong believer, immediately began to pray and give thanks. Remembering that experience, Bloom comments,

> In all my life I haven't been so grateful to God for any amount or quantity of food. I ate it as one would eat sacred food. I ate it carefully, not to miss any moment of this rich delight of the fresh cucumber, and after we had finished I had no hesitation in saying, "And now, let us give thanks to the Lord," and we started again in gratitude.[22]

In our weakness, God may teach us what is truly important. We may learn how to handle resources more effectively. We may learn that we can live on far less than we thought we could. Perhaps we may experience God's directing us to a new career or resources to help in our times of distress. There is no end to what God can accomplish in us when we reach out in all our brokenness and surrender our lives to our Lord.

The approach to you by someone experiencing financial distress often offers not only an opportune time to share Scripture verses and prayer with that person but also to direct him or her to resources that can help immensely in getting out of debt. One such resource consists in the program Financial Peace University, by Dave Ramsey. Many churches offer this program. Books and CDs/DVDs are also available for self-teaching. Generally, however, going through this process in a group is more helpful, supportive, and effective.

Financial stress and at times distress always lurk. When ministering to others experiencing these hardships, remember to listen, suggest helpful resources for overcoming financial distress, share Scripture, and always pray—in a sincere and sensitive manner, such as is demonstrated in the prayer below:

Dear Lord, help _____ (name) to find firm ground in an uncertain economy. As _____ (name) seeks work and assistance, give him/her strength not to be anxious when things seem to be going nowhere. Give _____ (name) patience not to despair when things look bleak; give _____ (name) serenity to know that you are right here, present with

---

[22] Anthony Bloom, *Beginning to Pray* (Paulist, 1970), 43.

him/her, helping to carry his/her cross each day. May _____ (name) do your will in all things that your holy name may be praised! Thank you, Lord, for all the ways that you care for and protect _____ (name). For all things we are truly grateful. Amen.

The Rev. Carolyn E. Cranston '99
Director of Alumnae/i and Church Relations

Helpful resources for further consultation include:

Beginning to Pray, Anthony Bloom (Paulist, 1970);

These biblical passages in particular: Psalm 46:1–3; Proverbs 19:21; Ecclesiastes 7:14; Luke 12:27–28; Philippians 4:6–7; 1 Thessalonians 5:16–18; James 1:5; 1 Peter 5:6–7;

Financial Peace University, Dave Ramsey, www.daveramsey.com/fpu;

www.beliefnet.com/prayers/protestant/work/prayer-for-help-with-finances.aspx; and

www.iprayprayer.com/prayers-money-prayers-finances-prayer-help-times-financial-hardship/.

NOTES

Forgiveness

There are times when we desire to be forgiven, and there are times when we need to forgive because we have been sinned against. In praying with and for someone experiencing the need for either one—or both—of these acts, a number of passages in the Bible can give us guidance and wisdom in knowing what to say and how to pray.

Seeking forgiveness is one of the greatest gifts a person can give to another and to her- or himself, for it has the potential to restore relationship and unburden both parties. Admitting one's need for forgiveness—"admitting you were wrong"—is also one of the most difficult acts. But the person who has knowingly offended another bears the responsibility of apologizing, whether or not that apology is fully received and forgiveness is given. Sometimes the offense is an infraction between just the individual and God. Such offenses, too, require the seeking of forgiveness, repentance, and changing one's course of action by rethinking how things should be done.

The following Scriptures will be helpful toward promoting healing and hope as you pray with and for someone who needs to seek forgiveness:

> If my people who are called by my name humble themselves, pray, seek my face, and turn from their wicked ways, then I will hear from heaven, and will forgive their sin and heal their land (2 Chron. 7:14).

> So if anyone is in Christ, there is a new creation: everything old has passed away; see, everything has become new (2 Cor. 5:17)!

> If we confess our sins, (God) who is faithful and just and will forgive us our sins and cleanse us from all unrighteousness (1 John 1:9).

To the person seeking forgiveness, offer the encouragement that God does not require of us a multiplicity of words, nor are many words necessary in humbly offering an apology to another person.

Depending on the seriousness of the offense from which a person is trying to recover, at the appropriate time in her or his healing process it may be important to suggest praying for the ability to forgive the offender—regardless of whether or not the offender has repented. The act of extending forgiveness is between the individual and God. It is a cleansing and unburdening of the forgiver's soul. It is the unraveling of hands and letting go. In order to progress in life by healthy means, the person who has been offended must, in time, let go of the control the offense has over her or him.

Since sometimes people are unable to grapple with offenses on their own, good counselors can help an offended person arrive at an emotionally healthy point to pray for the ability to forgive an offender. Sometimes encouraging the offended person to write down in a journal the name of the offender and what the offense may have been can be helpful in this process. Some people who practice such journaling also find it helpful to cross off the offense (or multiple offenses) as an outward demonstration of forgiveness—or even to burn the papers recording the painful event. For proper self-care, it is important consciously to acknowledge the offense as fully unacceptable and to establish healthy boundaries with the offender. At the right time, you might pray with the offended person that she or he will be able to forgive, learn any personal lessons, and then remember what she or he has learned through the difficult process.

The following Scriptures will be helpful toward promoting healing and hope as you pray with and for someone who needs to forgive another:

> For if you forgive others their trespasses, your heavenly Father will also forgive you (Matt. 6:14).
>
> Put away from you all bitterness and wrath and anger and wrangling and slander, together with all malice, and be kind to one another, tenderhearted, forgiving one another, as God in Christ has forgiven you (Eph. 4:31–32).
>
> Do not judge, and you will not be judged; do not condemn, and you will not be condemned. Forgive, and you will be forgiven (Luke 6:37).
>
> Father, forgive them; for they do not know what they are doing (Luke 23:34).

To hurting persons who are seeking the ability to forgive an offender, encourage their release of the offense against them.

This sample prayer uses language helpful for praying with persons seeking both to receive and to offer forgiveness:

Lord God, we know that you do not require us to use many words in humbly asking for or offering forgiveness. Please help _____ (name) to be able to say, simply, "I am sorry," both to you and to the person (she/he) has wronged. Show _____ (name) how to do better next time. Give (her/him) the courage to make this situation right. And give _____ (name) the courage to admit, "I am hurting," yet also to release the offense against (her/him). Help _____ (name) to let go perpetually and to grow from this hurtful situation. Amen.

The Rev. Kimberly R. Gonxhe '07
Director of the Metro-Urban Institute

Helpful resources for further consultation include:

> *A Beautiful Disaster: Finding Hope in the Midst of Brokenness*, by Marlena Graves (Brazos, 2014); and
>
> *Forgiveness: 21 Days to Forgive Everyone for Everything*, by Iyanla Vanzant (repr.; Smiley Books, 2017).

NOTES

GLOBAL CHURCH ISSUES

Whenever I return home to India, I am always asked questions about the church in the United States—questions such as, "How many Christians are there in the city you live in?" and "How is church attendance in the U.S.?" In fact, I get similar questions from friends here in the U.S. inquiring about Christians in my part of India. Christians from across the world are indeed intrigued to find out the state of Christian faith and practices in other parts of the world. I hope this interest comes not only out of our curiosity but also out of our deep sense of connection with our brothers and sisters who are trying to live faithfully to God within their own contexts.

When we start praying for the "global Church," we must examine what and who it is we tend to pray for. My guess is that most of us are praying for those in the southern hemisphere—the Global South, especially those countries experiencing poverty and social and political unrest. Witness the fact that many world prayer books focus on stories or problems from countries in the Global South and not in the Western world. This lopsidedness gives the impression that only the Church and people in Africa, Asia, and Latin America need our prayers.

While it is important that we pray for our brothers and sisters in these contexts, it sets up an unhelpful divide. This tendency to focus on praying for Christians in the Global South stems from the traditional perception that Christianity is a Western religion and that it spread globally from the West. Yet the truth is that Christianity had sprung out of Asia and spread through Asia and Africa long before it went to Western Europe (e.g., Acts 8:26–40). So in today's world, praying for the global Church doesn't necessarily mean only praying for the Church in India or Sierra Leone—it can also mean praying for the Church in the U.S. or Germany.

The need for prayer for churches throughout the world is further accented by the rapid growth of the Church in Latin America, Asia, and Africa. In all contexts—from north to south, east to west—faithful people are facing barriers, ranging from poverty to societal apathy, and political persecution to political exploitation of their faith. No matter how privileged the Church might be or appear to be in a given context, all Christian believers throughout the world need support in prayer by their brothers and sisters in Christ.

Furthermore, we pray for the global Church because Scripture instructs us to do so (1 Tim. 2:1). From a biblical perspective, we know that as Christians we are all connected as one in Jesus Christ. Paul in his letter to the Corinthian Church clearly states that, since we are all parts of the body of Christ, we cannot neglect some parts of the body and think they are not important or that we do not need them (1 Cor. 12:12–31). For Paul, if one part of the body suffers, the entire body suffers. We need each other in order to grow and learn.

Praying for the global Church can be difficult especially when we disagree with the particular beliefs of a specific church. According to the Center for the Study of Global Christianity, there are 45,000 Christian denominations in our world today.[23] Just imagine the number of theological differences and the varieties of ways we do church and mission. I myself find it tempting to start praying, "God, help these people see the light," which really means, "God, help these people figure out that I am right, and they are wrong." Yet the truth is that we should pray for God's truth and love to shine forth in all parts of the world even when doing so makes us uncomfortable.

Praying for the global Church can be overwhelming, too. There is so much going on in our world that we can get lost in who and what to pray for. But trying to be specific in our prayers can be very helpful at both ends. It can be done by finding a partner from the global Church, an individual, or a neighborhood community from a different culture or country where a mutual relationship can be established and mutual learning, sharing, and praying can be experienced by both sides.

So, as we pray for the global Church, let us remember that God is at work in different parts of the world, and together with our brothers and sisters around the world we are called to participate in God's work by praying together for God's reign in it. And let us begin by praying for the global Church:

God of all nations, whose name and glory are manifested through all the diversity of cultures, races, and languages all around the world: We confess, O God, that even though we know you have created everyone in your own image, oftentimes our words and actions deny this truth. Help us, O Lord, truly to see your face and hear your voice through the many faces and voices of our brothers and sisters around the world.

Lord, we pray for your Church throughout the world, that amid our differences we may realize we are all parts of one body. Give us the strength to love, to listen, to hear, to share our resources, and to work alongside those who think and worship you differently, knowing that there

---

[23] Todd M. Johnson and Cindy M. Wu, *Our Global Families: Christians Embracing Common Identity in a Changing World* (Baker Academic, 2015), 56.

is so much we can learn from one another and that together we can make your "Kin-dom" realized in this world. In Christ's name we pray. Amen.

The Rev. S. Balajiedlang (Bala) Khyllep
Associate Director of the World Mission Initiative

Helpful resources for further consultation include:

Global Church: Reshaping Our Conversations, Renewing Our Mission, Revitalizing Our Churches, by Graham Hill (IVP Academic, 2016);

"Globalization and the Global Church Part 2": https://outreachmagazine.com/interviews/41070-al-tizon-globalization-and-the-global-church-part-2.html;

Our Global Families: Christians Embracing Common Identity in a Changing World, by Todd M. Johnson and Cindy M. Wu (Baker Academic, 2015);

https://theglobalchurchproject.com/; and

http://worldinprayer.org/.

NOTES

Homelessness

Caring for and walking with those whose needs we cannot fill is part of the call and regular work of the Christian and pastor. We confess a God who is with us despite and in the midst of suffering, so we cannot be afraid to name God's presence even when things are beyond our power to repair.

Homelessness—the systems that cause it, the stigma it carries, and the combination of societal and circumstantial events that allow it to happen— are typically beyond our capacity to solve in our role as friend or even pastor. This reality is not to discourage our effort or in any way to take less seriously the words in James 2:15–17,

> If a brother or sister is naked and lacks daily food, and one of you says to them, "Go in peace; keep warm and eat your fill," and yet you do not supply their bodily needs, what is the good of that? So faith by itself, if it has no works, is dead.

That said, these words, alongside our own tendency to live by shame rather than grace, have through time tempted Christians to fear and ignore people facing or experiencing homelessness—for we know, deep down somewhere, that a sister or a brother suffering in such a way is an indictment of the society we participate in and the comparative luxury in which we shelter ourselves. Encountering those who are suffering for lack of material comforts is encountering our own privilege, and that encounter is difficult. Even further, prayer in such a space is particularly difficult, because in prayer we are coming before the God of truth, and the truth is that we are not living in a just system.

So the first question is, "How can I pray in the midst of injustice?" or perhaps more accurately, "How can I pray honestly for my and our rescue from a culture of death, even as I, as a housed person, am on the winning side of that culture?" We can be tempted to think that praying about homelessness is about our praying for others; but our prayer must actually start with our own healing. And that prayer, more likely than not, starts with the silence of listening—for God and for the stories of those we journey alongside.

Many of us have never experienced the anxiety and trauma of being homeless or precariously housed. As with any difficult circumstance, the trauma of homelessness is layered. Socially, homeless persons are viewed differently, avoided, ignored, and exiled from community life. Physically, they are vulnerable—not only to the elements but also to unhealthy food, unsanitary conditions, and the stealing from them of what little they have while they sleep. Emotionally, they are forced to contend with loss, hazards, and systems that are foreign to the majority of people who pass by them every day.

When working and praying with people in these vulnerable circumstances, know that they are the experts. Ask them what they would like to pray for. Take them seriously when they tell you. Listen to their stories and share stories of your own. Do not, as the victor in this culture of death, try to train or invite them to be more like you. Learn from them how to pray. After all, if we are praying the prayer Christ taught us to pray, it will be in the words of a man who had "nowhere to lay his head" (Luke 9:58).

The prayer below uses language that follows the guidance given here:

God who traveled in our behalf, be with your servant _____ (name), who traveled in our behalf to join us here. Thank you for the love you have shown us in our time with _____ (name), for we are always blessed when your beloved come to us. Holy Spirit, Hedge of Protection, Comforter, walk with _____ (name), stand guard over her/him as she/he sleeps and bless her/his steps as she/he wakes to go where you call her/him. God, when hope is wearing thin, stand with _____ (name). Wherever she/he goes, stay with her/him, for we know that wherever she/he is, she/he will always be within the reach of your voice, your grace, and your love. And we pray that _____ (name) might come back safely to meet us again.

Further, loving God, we pray for our world and our culture. We ask that you would continue to knit us into relationship with one another, that we might bear each other's burdens, comfort each other's sorrows, and celebrate each other's joys. Jesus, we know that we are more whole when we stand with each other. Strengthen us to do just that when seasons are hard. We trust that we are yours. May we practice the unity of sisterhood and brotherhood together all our lives long—in this place and beyond it. Amen.

The Rev. Karen Rohrer
Director of the Church Planting Initiative

Helpful resources for further consultation include:

Evicted: Poverty and Profit in the American City, by Matthew Desmond (Broadway Books, 2017);

"Facts on Homelessness," https://projecthome.org/about/facts-homelessness; and

Nickle and Dimed: On (Not) Getting by in America, by Barbara Ehrenreich (Picador, 2011).

NOTES

ILLNESS AND HEALING

Healing in the biblical sense means to be restored to wholeness and thereby become a full participant in communal life, thus manifesting that the reign of God has come near. Jesus understood his mission as restoring humanity and all creation to the fullness of life: "I came that they may have life, and have it abundantly" (John 10:10b). God desires our abundant wholeness in all dimensions of life: physical, emotional, social, moral, and spiritual. As we open to and follow the life-giving way of Jesus as manifested in his life, death, and resurrection, we move toward the ever greater wholeness that God wants to give us individually and corporately. Likewise, when we move toward separation, loss of moral and spiritual integrity, or destruction, we know illness. The forces of life and death struggle within all of us individually and in our communities and in our nations. How then do we pray for healing?

There are many ways Christians pray for healing when we or our loved ones become afflicted with an illness that may be temporary, chronic, critical, and possibly final. Underlying any form of prayer for healing in the Gospels is the genuineness of the faith of the one asking for healing—healing for oneself (e.g., blind Bartimaeus in Mark 10:46–52; the leper in Luke 5:12–16; the hemorrhaging woman in Mark 5:25–35) or another person (e.g., Jairus's daughter in Matt. 9:18–26; the Roman centurion's servant in Luke 7:1–10; the paralytic in Luke 5:17–26). Three deeply interrelated components are involved in faith: *fides quae*, "faith that" is believed—namely, the content of faith revealed through sacred Scripture and expressed in doctrines and rituals held and taught by the church; *fides qua*, the "faith by which" a person is empowered to respond to God and which includes the person's understanding of self in relation to God, as well as her or his own filtered view of the content of faith; and *fidelitas*, "faithfulness" in setting one's heart on whom she or he has believed, due to the character, ability, strength, or truth of God and God's promises.

In my pastoral encounters with those who are dealing with chronic or serious illnesses, I engage them in simple conversation that explores three intersecting relationships: how they view their illness, how they describe their relationship to God and God's relationship to them and their illness, and what it means for them to be healed or made whole. I listen for their particular ways of speaking of God, who God is for them, their beliefs and feelings about their illness, their desires for healing and wholeness. I listen for images and metaphors that may arise in the conversation. Then I wonder with them if God's Spirit, whose power is at work in them, could be leading them to a deeper wholeness than they could possibly ask for or even imagine (see Eph. 3:20, "Now to him who by the power at work within us is able to accomplish abundantly far more than all we can ask or imagine"). Whatever arises from this conversation gives me a way to pray for healing for and with them as I draw upon some of their God language, images, metaphors, and desires for wholeness—including the wholeness that is beyond what we can ask for or even imagine that God has promised to give to those who wholeheartedly entrust themselves and their concerns to God.

In a pastoral conversation I had with a woman who was fighting for survival as she dealt with a life-threatening diagnosis, she told me she felt as though she had entered a room that was totally dark. She could not see anything in the room, did not know where she was, and was afraid to take another step for fear there was no floor and she would fall into an abyss. I asked her whether she could imagine herself in that darkness lifting just one foot forward very carefully to see what would happen. After a long pause, she closed her eyes and gripped the arms of the chair to do just that—to see what would happen if, in her mind, she lifted that foot. As she engaged in this exercise, her face showed signs of struggle and then some release. She expressed surprise as she said, "the floor seemed to rise up to meet my foot." After taking several more steps in her imagination, she reflected aloud, "So this is what faith really is: it's trusting that God will be there meeting me in every step, even though I cannot see the floor or know where I'm going!" This image and metaphor of faith arising out of our pastoral conversation became the focus of our prayer together:

Gracious God, you have shown us that even in the darkest of times, you are there meeting us precisely where we are most vulnerable. In Christ you have embraced our fear and suffering and empowered us to take one step at a time toward the wholeness that is deeper than what we can ask for or even imagine. May we proclaim the power of your Spirit at work in us, and may we hold fast to your gift of life given to us this day, for your glory. Amen.

Dr. Martha A. Robbins
Joan Marshall Associate Professor Emerita of Pastoral Care and
Director of the Pneuma Institute

Helpful resources for further consultation include:

> *Dreams: God's Forgotten Language*, by John A. Sanford (HarperOne, 1989);
>
> *Prayers for Every Need*, by William H. Kadel (C. D. Deans, 1966); and
>
> *Prayers for Help and Healing*, by William Barclay (Augsburg, 1995).

NOTES

INCARCERATION

There are three groups of people affected by incarceration we should think about when we pray: the currently incarcerated, the formerly incarcerated, and the families of both. The following information is helpful to keep in mind when praying with or for individuals in these groups.

One non-celebratory fact is that the United States has the highest prison population and the second highest incarceration rate of any country in the world. More than 2 million people are in prison in this country, and more than 7 million are under correctional control, at an estimated cost to taxpayers of $80 billion per year. More money is spent on maintaining a prisoner than on educating a child. Over the course of 30 years, the United States has been building the prison industrial complex as specifically linked to the "war on drugs." According to research, however, drug use in this country was in decline when our government declared this war.

Moreover, this mass incarceration system disfavors people of color. Michelle Alexander notes in her book, *The New Jim Crow*, that there are more African-Americans in prison, on parole, or on probation than there were slaves in the earlier centuries of U.S. history. Further, juveniles comprise an often-overlooked population in our prisons. The United States is one of only a few countries that have incarcerated juveniles for life. Some of them are even on death row.

For prisoners who do not receive lifetime sentences, life after release is different. Many return to a world much different from the one they remembered as existing prior to their imprisonment. In their "new" world, many are denied job opportunities, public housing, and in some jurisdictions the right to vote. Both during and after their incarceration, the effects of their imprisonment are not limited to the prisoners themselves—their families and communities are also affected. As Christians, our faithfulness to the gospel requires us to become aware that U.S. laws were constructed in such a way as to disadvantage unfairly one group of people over another. These same laws are the source of the disproportionality in both sentencing and ethnic representation in our prisons.

When providing pastoral care to the incarcerated, the formerly incarcerated, and their families, it is important not to pass judgment—for recall that the Bible itself records multiple imprisonments that were unjust. We see in Genesis 39 that Joseph was wrongly imprisoned, and we read in Jeremiah 37 that Jeremiah suffered the same injustice. We learn of the unjust imprisonment of John the Baptist in Matthew 11, of Paul and Silas in Acts 16, and of Paul's final arrest and wrongful imprisonment beginning in Acts 21. And in all four of the Gospels we read of the Lord Jesus' arrest, imprisonment, and sentencing—the quintessential example of legal injustice (see Matthew 26–27, Mark 14–15, Luke 22–23, and John 18). Excepting in the account of John the Baptist, we see explicitly in all these cases that the one imprisoned made a positive impact on the others in the prison community—prisoners and prison workers alike.

Matthew 25:36 reminds us of our obligation to visit those who are in prison. But the word for "visit" used in this passage—*episketomai*—carries with it the connotation of caring for, looking upon in order to benefit. It does not mean simply peeking in on. Whether a prisoner was justly found guilty or wrongfully accused and convicted, we are called upon to care for him or her. And in our offering of active care to the imprisoned, we ought to hope that such care becomes contagious among that population, beginning with the people we are caring for and spreading to their fellow prisoners.

Then, when an incarcerated individual is released, we need to extend our help further in the reunification process with his or her family and in the reintegration process into the community. Our active and prayerful support as the former prisoner adjusts to regained freedom can play an essential role in a good and positive outcome for all involved.

Consider using language such as that in the prayer below when praying with a current or former prisoner, his or her family, and your congregation, Bible study group, or circle of friends:

God of Heaven and earth and all that is therein, give us the compassion to care for those bound in our prison system. Help us to look beyond the crime just as you look beyond our faults. Help us to see the person imprisoned as someone created in your image and in your likeness, and help us to respond to his/her humanity. God, I pray for the ones who have been set free, having served their time, that their road to reintegration would be made smooth by an array of opportunities—opportunities that will allow them to have their dignity restored. For you, O Lord, saw enough in all of us, as ill-deserving as we were, to give your life on our behalf. Thank you for your love that allowed mercy to cover us and grace to keep us, even from ourselves. Amen.

The Rev. Dr. John C. Welch '02
Vice President for Student Services and Community Engagement and Dean of Students

Helpful resources for further consultation include:

Just Mercy, by Brian Stevenson (Random House, 2014);

Ministry to the Incarcerated, by Henry G. Covert (Amazon Digital, 2014); and

The New Jim Crow, by Michelle Alexander (The New Press, 2012).

Incarcerated persons might wish to consult:

From the Bottom of the Heap: The Autobiography of Black Panther Robert Hillary King, by Robert Hillary King (rev. exp. ed.; PM Press, 2012);

The Sun Does Shine: How I Found Life and Freedom on Death Row, by Anthony Ray Hinton with Lara Love Hardin (St. Martin's, 2018); and

https://www.prisonfellowship.org/resources/training-resources/in-prison/ministry-basics/what-bible-says-about-prison-ministry/.

Families of the incarcerated will find helpful materials at:

https://www.prisonfellowship.org/resources/support-friends-family-of-prisoners/coping-incarceration-loved-one/.

On the topic of justice reform, see:

https://www.prisonfellowship.org/resources/justice-reform-resources/.

NOTES

Injustice

Unfortunately, the day may come when those we love and shepherd will personally encounter injustice. Providing pastoral care in those long seasons is fraught with challenge. The range of emotions experienced by individuals and groups when denied justice is different from the sting of life's disappointments or the introspection born from personal failings—for when communities encounter injustice they experience evil.

Those who practice injustice fundamentally deny human dignity and worth. People experiencing the governmental corruption that robs dignity and denies flourishing to its citizens can feel desperate for the arrival of change. Individuals suffering under leadership that fails to protect young and old from the ravages of violence can lead to feelings of powerless in the face of fear. And communities entangled in evil systems designed to channel resources to certain citizens while denying those same opportunities to others can be ravaged with despair. These perverse denials of human dignity can lead to such intense reactions because the evils can seem unrelenting.

We were not intended to live with injustice, for God is the author of justice! The message for those being denied justice—whether through economic oppression, denial of human rights, unjust lawsuits, or even deceptive plots—is that they are in solidarity with the Lord whenever they long for justice. For God, the author of grace, is just and insists that we be just. In Scripture, God demonstrated this truth by setting apart a people to belong to God and telling the people, "Justice, and only justice, you shall pursue" (Deut. 16:20). In other words, justice was a requisite for living in relationship with God and one another. Justice was meant to be at the forefront of the community, so when cultures of injustice arose, God would send prophets to call for justice to "roll down like waters, and righteousness like an ever-flowing stream" (Amos 5:24). The people were to "do justice, and to love kindness, and to walk humbly with [their] God" (Micah 6:8), because God delights in justice. Longing for our countries and communities to be places filled with justice puts us in union with our God, who is always just.

When praying with individuals who experience injustice and its attendant feelings of desperation, powerlessness, and despair, we are invited to remember the principles found in Psalm 37, for they address the question of how to maintain one's integrity in the face of injustice. This psalm of King David counsels, "Do not fret because of the wicked; do not be envious of wrongdoers, for they will soon fade like the grass, and wither like the green herb" (vv. 1–2). Injustice can distort the vision of its victims by tempting them to magnify the power of the unjust. But the psalmist reminds those longing for justice that, despite appearances, the wicked are as fragile as grass and as temporary as spring sprouts.

The writer of Psalm 37 encourages those who long for justice to remember the Lord's power and promise to right wrongs: God "will make your vindication shine like the light, and the justice of your cause like the noonday [sun]" (v. 6). Further, righteous victims of injustice can find solace from knowing that "the LORD laughs at the wicked," for God "sees that their day is coming" (v. 13). Despite the appearance that wicked and ruthless people are well established, they can disappear from the midst of the righteous without warning; therefore, the psalmist invites those presently denied justice to forsake a posture of worry, fret, and envy of the evil people, plans, and systems aligned against them. Psalm 37 cautions against the harm that can come from meeting injustice with anger and rage: "Depart from evil, and do good" (v. 27a), "Wait for the LORD, and keep to [God's] way" (v. 34a)—so the poem shows mindfulness that we, too, can become poisoned by the denial of justice and turn to unjust actions ourselves. God's people must not and cannot fight injustice with the power of rage.

Instead, God's justice-seeking people can pray these words as we march toward halls of corruption or enter places of evil power: "the LORD loves justice; [God] will not forsake his faithful ones" (v. 28). And as we continually remind one another who we are—*and Whose we are*—with the psalmist we declare, "Our steps are made firm by the LORD, when [God] delights in our way; though we stumble, we shall not fall headlong, for the LORD holds us by the hand" (vv. 23–24).

The following Wesleyan prayer invites all those who are denied justice to persevere in integrity:

God, righteous and enduring: Look with pity upon those who grow weary and discouraged in their work for justice. When it seems to them that nothing ever changes for the better, that the forces of evil will always prevail, remind them that you, the Almighty, have endured not years or decades of resistance, but whole centuries and indeed millennia. Yet you promise that your righteousness will triumph, that evil will collapse. Save the tired strivers after justice from the doom of Sisyphus: daily hoisting a mighty rock up a high hill, only to have it tumble down again. Assure them that the stones they move, by grace will be assembled into a house of righteousness upon the highest of the mountains, and that all the peoples of the earth shall stream too it, that all may walk in the ways of the Lord. Grant this through Jesus, the chief foundation stone. Amen.[24]

The Rev. Ayana H. Teter
Director of Vocational Discernment

Helpful resources for further consultation include:

> *Conversations with God: Two Centuries of Prayers by African Americans*, by James M. Washington (Harperperennial, 1995); and
>
> *Long Walk To Freedom: The Autobiography of Nelson Mandela*, by Nelson Mandela (Back Bay Books/ Little, Brown and Company, 1995).

---

[24] Laurence Hull Stookey, *This Day: A Wesleyan Way of Prayer* (Abingdon, 2004), 151.

NOTES

Internet Abuse

It is difficult to keep track of the groundbreaking papers, blogs, studies, and articles that cover the dangers of screen time and abuses of the Internet among teens and children. But Internet abuses are not limited to kids. There is no shortage of tragic abuse committed by adults. How does it happen? Often, it just creeps in nearly unnoticed.

For example, it can be so frustrating when something stubbornly stays on the tip of your tongue. Whatever the subject, there is something deeply unsettling when you can't quite recall that one, unimportant thing. The name of that catchy song. The other movie that actress is in. The city with that really cool thing you saw a while back. The team we played in the play-offs five years ago. In today's world, though, it takes only a few seconds to retrieve that one, unimportant thing. A quick search on your phone, laptop, tablet, game system, or even TV will provide you with the answer. Access to information is virtually ubiquitous. But it comes at a price.

Strangely enough, the ability to access that one, unimportant thing— that thing we're frequently trying to use in building a communicative relationship with someone else—often comes at the *price* of our relationships. Our relationships with other people, certainly, and also our relationship with God. Or at least "access-ability" *can* come at that price.

The ability to retrieve that one, unimportant thing can cost us our relationships because, in addition to searching the Internet for nearly all-things-informational, we can do or encounter many relationship-damaging, even relationship-destroying things. Bullying, identity theft, addiction to pornography, digital piracy, misuse of social media, and myriad other abuses are now possible from a device we keep in our pockets. And naturally, our devices also make it much easier simply to ignore the people who are physically in our presence.

When we minister to those who are affected by some form of Internet abuse—including over-use and addiction—it is wise to remember that Internet abuses can range in severity from occasional rudeness to unwise, habitual, unethical, and even illegal activity. Prayer is appropriate in each case. Referral to additional professional help may also be necessary in serious situations.

Of course, the devices and the access they provide are really just tools. We may find it convenient to blame the Internet for the adverse results of its abuse, but ultimately such scapegoating isn't helpful. If a marriage breaks up because of a spouse's addiction to pornography on "the Net," if depression intensifies through relational reliance on social media, or if a loved one suffers cyber-bullying, blaming the medium may offer a quick hit of self-righteous rationalization, but doing so won't—and can't—offer lasting healing.

Instead of focusing on the tool, therefore, it may be more helpful to identify its impact on our relationships. Praying for the relationships adversely affected by our abuse of technology not only restores our communion with God and invites God into those human relationships but also forces us to consider the people around us. As we pray for and with people suffering from Internet abuse—whether as abusers or victims of its abuse—we must be both respectful and honest. One's actions online affect the lives of real human beings—the individual user's included. By naming that fact out loud in prayer, we can ask the Holy Spirit to strengthen and heal relationships as well as begin addressing the abuse itself.

The following prayer provides language for praying about this important challenge in our technology-saturated world:

Holy Spirit, we ask you to mend our broken relationships. Open our eyes to the people you have placed in our lives and heal the hurts caused by our actions. Restore us to a right relationship with you and with one another. Show us how to use the tools available to us to draw close to one another and to you. Teach us to use our abilities for your purposes. In Jesus' name we pray. Amen.

The Rev. Derek R. Davenport '05/'17
Director of the Miller Summer Youth Institute

Helpful resources for further consultation include:

> *Beyond the Screen: Youth Ministry for the Connected but Alone Generation*, by Andrew Zirschky (Abingdon, 2015);

> *Cyber Junkie: Escape the Gaming and Internet Trap*, by Kevin J. Roberts (Hezelden, 2010);

Virtual Addiction: Help for Netheads, Cyberfreaks, and Those Who Love Them, by David N. Greenfield (New Harbinger, 1999);

www.stopbullyging.gov; and

www.virtual-addiction.com.

NOTES

Job Loss

"What do you want to be when you grow up?" This question, posed to generations of children, almost invariably assumes one kind of answer—what kind of occupation do you want to have? In it, we are not asking about the ways of relating to others or practices or kinds of values that mark adulthood; rather, we expect an answer such as teacher, firefighter, doctor, or the like. I remember my son's pushing back against an essay he had been assigned to write in school; asked what he wanted to do as an adult, he was at a loss. I queried, "What do you want to do?" He replied, "All I want is to make a positive difference."

The connection between our occupations and our identity is deeply embedded in our pragmatic American culture. Who we are and what we do for a living don't quite make a perfectly overlapping Venn diagram, but it's close. Think about the prevailing rhetoric around education: it does not center on preparing thoughtful members of the civic community—it centers on preparing people for participation in the workplace. Bookstores and libraries have dozens of linear feet of shelf space dedicated to getting your dream job, following your passion, and taking charge of your professional life. And most religious communities explicitly affirm the importance of work that is adequately compensated, meaningful, and dignified.

But the reality is that we live in a time marked by a volatile economy, uncertainty about the future, and dramatic shifts in the marketplace. This changeable environment means that, for most people, work is less likely to be an exercise in self-actualization and more likely a means by which they can take care of themselves and their dependents and possibly have a sense of place in the world—and an increasingly unreliable means at that. When people lose their jobs (or can't seem to land a job in the first place), it is often for reasons that are out of their control. In short, there is a deep schism between popular and theological ideas about work and the day-to-day lived experience of it.

When doing pastoral care among people who have lost their jobs and perhaps experienced a crisis in vocation, it is important to address the complex set of feelings and consequences of job loss. Being out of work can be devastating at many levels. Most obviously, there is a loss of income and a means to care for self and family. This pragmatic loss can be compounded by a personal sense of shame and loss of identity, worth, and place in the community. Some newly jobless people might even call into question their sense of God's faithfulness.

One of the most important things to do pastorally with people who have experienced job loss is to give them space to process the full range of strong emotions that are likely to be part of the experience. They need to be able to speak their truth. Simple maxims such as "God has a plan" or "God won't give you more than you can handle" can be received as patronizing and do not honor the real feelings of anxiety and anger that are likely present, along with the difficult circumstances their loved ones are experiencing as well. These easy one-liners can increase the sense of loss and frustration, thus causing a person to feel even more distant from a God whose plan involves suffering or whose intent is unclear. Instead, it is important to affirm the jobless where they are and to witness that God desires their flourishing.

It is also important to help nurture the resilience that will be crucial in their moving forward; regaining employment is itself hard work. The Psalms of Lament—particularly Psalm 77—can help here; as the people of Israel felt abandoned by God, they gave full voice to their anger with God: "In the day of my trouble I seek the Lord; in the night my hand is stretched out without wearying; my soul refuses to be comforted" (v. 2). And yet these psalms end with hymns of praise and wonder: "You led your people like a flock by the hand of Moses and Aaron" (v. 20). What helped the psalmist make the shift? Remembering God's faithfulness and telling the stories of God's abiding presence through other trials.

Part of pastoral work with people struggling as a result of job loss, then, can involve praying these psalms. Doing so might take the form of an exercise such as Dwelling in the Word, which would ask the people praying to meditate on where they resonate with the experience of the Israelites and where they see God's presence in and absence from their own lives. Invite them to remember, as the psalmist does, stories of God's provision and, recalling their own gifts and talents, the parts of them that contribute to their communities. If hope and trust in God's faithfulness seem to be beyond their reach, then it can be the role of the pastoral caregiver to promise them to carry that hope and trust until they are able to do so themselves.

A similar exercise can be done with the call of Abram and Sarai (Gen. 12:1), whom God calls from the familiar and the comfortable and asks to pull up stakes and "go to the land that I will show you." As people confront the revisioning of their vocation, this story can help them to name their own feelings of fear and uncertainty in the midst of loss and to frame those feelings with a narrative of God's faithfulness even in the midst of the unknown.

Both exercises may be closed by praying with persons in this uncertain position—praying for provision and peace and for the capacity to see the next area, opportunity, or situation to which they are called. If they are part of your community of faith, it might even be helpful to pray with the sufferer that the community of believers be present to their fellow member's loss and material need. The following prayer, attributed to St. Francis de Sales in the late 16th century, may be helpful:

Do not look forward in fear to the changes of life;
Rather look to them with full hope that as they arise, God, whose very own you are, will lead you safely through all things;
And when you cannot stand it, God will carry you in His arms.
Do not fear what may happen tomorrow;
The same everlasting Father who cares for you today will take care of you today and every day.
He will either shield you from suffering or will give you unfailing strength to bear it.
Be at peace and put aside all anxious thoughts and imaginations.

Dr. Helen M. Blier
Director of Continuing Education

Helpful resources for further consultation include:

> *Learning to Walk in the Dark*, by Barbara Brown Taylor (HarperOne, 2015);

> *Leaving Church: A Memoir of Faith*, by Barbara Brown Taylor (HarperOne, 2009);

> *Let Your Life Speak*, by Parker Palmer (Jossey-Bass, 1999);

> *Rising Strong*, by Brene Brown (Random House, 2017); and

> *Threshold of Discovery: A Field Guide to Spirituality in Midlife*, by L. Roger Owens (Church Publishing, 2017).

Notes

Mental Illness

Caring for and walking with those whose hurt we cannot heal is part of the calling of all who follow Christ. We do not worship a God of quick fixes—we confess a God who is with us despite and in the midst of suffering, so we cannot be afraid to name God's presence even when things are difficult.

Mental Illness, from the minor to the severe, affects the people we encounter, no matter what our context. How do we pray with and for them?

First, we cannot be afraid to name what so many other cultural forces invite us to ignore. Speaking of suicidal ideation, addiction, PTSD, depression, and other forms of mental illness is important in our personal conversations and in our worship spaces if we are honestly to invite people to bring their whole selves into Christian community. Simply naming these realities as hurts and pains at work in the world goes a long way. Removing the blame from the conversation and, instead, acknowledging and seeking God as the source of hope and freedom invites people to speak of their pain without feeling they are blamed or at fault, unlike what so often happens in other relationships and spaces.

In the recovery process from mental illness, certain terms are often used in teaching individuals how they might work toward health. Familiarizing oneself with these terms, used by communities of mental-health providers, can go a long way toward writing and praying helpful prayers for those in the recovery process. Language such as "one day at a time," "using your best thinking," and praying for the "strength to do the work" can be constructive for people who are not sure whether they, in their experience as persons who are healing rather than healed, are welcome.

In addition to being mindful of language, it is helpful for the one ministering to seek out prayers, poems, and first-person accounts that speak to the experience of those suffering from mental illness. Offering words to pray that feel honest and authentic can be a great gift to people who have been taught that their suffering and frustration are somehow wrong or are not the sorts of issues they should bring before God and the Christian community. The Psalms are rich in such resources (see, for example, Psalms 88 and 139), as are the writings of the mystics—Julian of Norwich's *Showings*, for example—and both types of resources can be adapted for liturgical use in prayers that focus on mental illness and community discipleship. For a more modern conversation, Kathryn Green-McCreight's book *Darkness Is My Only Companion: A Christian Response to Mental Illness* is a rich resource for those who are suffering from mental illness, for their caregivers, for the community, and for the minister/pastor. All these resources point us away from the dangerous notion that there is an easy answer to the issues involved in mental illness and recovering from it.

As we welcome those in our midst who are suffering, it is also important to consider the ways this welcoming might affect the rest of the community. Congregants learn from their leadership how to talk with those suffering from mental illness and how to pray for and engage the topic of mental illness. They also learn boundaries from their leadership. While we are certainly called to care for and walk with those who suffer, we must also remember our call to serve the church body as a whole. That call may require prohibiting certain behaviors and confronting individuals, even individuals who are suffering. In all this work, remembering and naming that God is God and we are not (in prayer and beyond prayer) allows us to care for those who suffer while also maintaining our focus on community discipleship and mutual support, rather than creating a minister-savior complex in ourselves or teaching people who are suffering that nothing is expected of them in terms of community life and discipleship.

A prayer that recognizes the pain suffered in mental illness while at the same time holding hope in God might be:

God who goes with us, even into the depths, we have been afraid that our despair is too deep for grace and we have fallen too far from redemption. Our pain has disrupted our best thinking, pulled us away from loved ones, and left us isolated from the understanding and compassion we crave. Even in community, we feel lonely and frightened. Holy Spirit, we find a companion as we pray with the psalmist, while trusting that even in our anger you have promised to meet us with love.

> *O LORD, why do you cast me off? Why do you hide your face from me?*
> *Wretched and close to death from my youth up, I suffer your terrors; I am desperate.*
> *Your wrath has swept over me; your dread assaults destroy me.*
> *They surround me like a flood all day long; from all sides they close in on me.*
> *You have caused friend and neighbor to shun me; my companions are in darkness.*[25]

---

[25] Psalm 88:14–18.

Loving God, we read in Scripture that "even the darkness is not dark to you."[26] Recall to us your light, so that we might find our footing again. Amen.

The Rev. Karen Rohrer
Director of the Church Planting Initiative

Helpful resources for further consultation include:

> *Blessed are the Crazy: Breaking Silence about Mental Illness, Family and Church*, by Sarah Griffith Lund (Chalice, 2014);
>
> *Darkness is my Only Companion: A Christian Response to Mental Illness*, by Kathryn Greene-McCreight (Brazos, 2015);
>
> *Delight in Disorder: Ministry, Madness, Mission*, by Tony E. Roberts (Way With Words, 2014);
>
> *Grace for the Afflicted*, by Matthew S. Stanford (IVP, 2017);
>
> *Madness: American Protestant Responses to Mental Illness*, by Heather H. Vacek (Baylor University Press, 2015);
>
> *On Edge: Mental Illness in the Christian Context*, by Kristin Kansiewicz (CreateSpace, 2014); and
>
> *Troubled Minds: Mental Illness and the Church's Mission*, by Amy Simpson and Marshall Shelley (IVP, 2013).

---

[26] Psalm 139:12.

Notes

Murder and Terrorism

Praying is difficult. In one of the most significant texts in the Bible, Paul writes, "the Spirit helps us in our weakness; for we do not know how to pray as we ought" (Rom. 8:26). In our most honest moments, even as we are praying we might admit this truth. We ought to pray, so we do. But how often do we reflect deeply and honestly about what we are doing?

Long predating people's spurning of public "thoughts and prayers" as pointless cliché in the face of gun violence and terrorism, Christians have prayed before, during, and after tragic events that have devastated life in spheres private, regional, national, and global. But even though prayer is one of the central acts of our faith, many Christians pray without spending much time thinking about what prayer is and about the many questions that pertain to praying. Why should one pray—and what kind of prayer? Who should pray—and for whom? When should one pray—and where? How should one pray—for how long and how often? Praying is both natural and difficult, especially when heartbreaking calamity strikes hard and near, as it does when murder and terrorism touch a person's life.

Following Jesus' teaching and example we pray, "Your will be done" (Matt. 6:10; 26:42). But ordinarily we ask God to change the circumstances in which we find ourselves or the world—perhaps partly because it is so difficult to discern God's will for us, for others, and our world. Despite our best intentions, in our praying we really mean, "Please grant what I wish for me, for others, and for the world." We pray as though to bend God's will toward our hopes and desires—desires that seem to us to follow our understanding of God's will for peace and the well-being of all people. But notwithstanding all the prayers we offer, the world goes on in a way that reminds us we are not in control of what happens, no matter how much we pray. We might even recognize that our prayers unwittingly indicate our acknowledgment of that reality; that is to say, the very effort to exert our will and effect our desires through prayer—with God's blessing, of course—is a way of expressing our helplessness and hopelessness.

How authentic of Paul and how salutary for us, then, for him to say, "that very Spirit intercedes with sighs too deep for words" (Rom. 8:26). Sometimes sighs too deep for words may be the best kind of prayer. We can find examples of "silence as prayer" in both the Bible and subsequent Christian tradition (the monastic practice of silence, and contemplative prayers, for example); one of the best illustrations comes in Job 2:11–13, which depicts how Job's three friends respond to his ineffable suffering. The entire pericope deserves lengthy reflection and can teach us much about compassion and prayer, but as regards prayer with others about murder and terrorism, note particularly the final verse: "They sat with him on the ground seven days and seven nights, and no one spoke a word to him, for they saw that his suffering was very great."

With all these preparatory considerations, inadequate as they are, we will find it hard to pray about murder—the intentional taking of human life by another human being—and terrorism—the unlawful use of violence and intimidation, especially against civilians, in the pursuit of political aims. Murder and acts of terrorism instill fear in a person or society through violent acts. Even more burdensome than the violence itself is the human agency involved: for every murder and act of terrorism, there is a murderer and a terrorist, whether acting alone or with others.

And for all who are affected by murder and terrorism, there follow some of the strongest human emotions: grief, anger, and fear. Without neglecting these strong feelings in ourselves and in others, it helps to take a deep breath, the very breath that marked the beginning of human life (Gen. 2:7), and to sigh deeply as we meditate and pray—pray to find inner peace, pray to be transformed even by such tragedies into more compassionate people who are mindful of others' suffering:

> Lord, make me an instrument of your peace. Where there is hatred, let me sow love, . . . Where there is despair, hope; . . . O divine Master, Grant that I may not so much seek to be consoled, as to console, to be understood, as to understand, to be loved, as to love (from The Prayer of St. Francis).

With sensitivity to the appropriate time for interceding with others who have experienced the tragedies of murder and terrorism, our compassion and sympathy must go in at least two directions—though in many cases and for many of us, reluctantly so. Clearly, Christians will not differ from others in being shaken by the fact of murder as also of an act of terrorism. But as Christians we must love our enemies and pray for those who persecute us (Matt. 5:44). There are, therefore, at least three parties with whom it is appropriate to pray: the two sets of victims of every act of murder and terrorism, namely, the direct target(s) of a violent act, and those related to or directly affected by the violence—family members, friends, a town; and third, as difficult as it is to accept, the perpetrator of the murder and/or terrorism, who bears the same *imago Dei* as the victims and ourselves (Gen. 1:26–27). Beyond these parties, prayer for a fourth element is appropriate: the very act of violence that is murder and terrorism—constant companions throughout human history.

The most difficult prayer task might be that of praying *with* a murderer or terrorist—a Christian vocation for prison chaplains, to be sure; but all Christians can at least pray for those who are called to pray with murderers and terrorists. Private prayer in the way of Job's friends—that is, prayer in the presence of those who suffer—can be helpful for those affected by murder and terrorism; so also can prayer that is somewhat "distanced" from the tragedies and the people involved in them—prayer in communities of faith, during congregational worship, in prayer circles, in Bible study groups, and in the public square, if appropriate.

Murder is the first crime recorded in the Bible (Gen. 4:8)—a crime for which human beings have found no earthly remedy. Acts of terrifying violence appear throughout the pages of the Old and New Testaments. As long as murder and terrorism are human realities, Christians must pray alongside victims as well as perpetrators with sighs too deep for words. Such is the mission and calling of those who follow the One crucified on the cross, a victim of murder and terror, whose death authenticates God's love and the Good News embodied in the risen Jesus Christ.

I have found Anthony Bloom's *Beginning to Pray* to be one of the most insightful and helpful books for my own reflections on prayer. In praying with people whose lives have been touched by murder and terrorism, consider the silent presence of the friends of Job. When words are appropriate, a prayer such as the one below might usher a measure of comfort:

(Prepare with slow, deep breathing.)
Lord of life, have mercy on us and grant us peace. Hear the cries of your children who have been shaken by the horror of violence and the loss of human life. As we grieve with sighs too deep for words, grant us strength to trust in your love to surround our fear and anger. Grant us compassion for those who caused so much anguish; may they also know your love for them. Heal us all and make us whole; make us instruments of your peace and love, through Jesus Christ. Amen.

The Rev. Dr. Kang-Yup Na
Member of the Board of Directors and
Associate Professor of Religion, Westminster College (New Wilmington, Pa.)

Helpful resources for further reading include:

If God is Good: Faith in the Midst of Suffering and Evil, by Randy Alcorn (Multnomah, 2014);

The Problem of Pain, by C. S. Lewis (rev. ed.; HarperOne, 2015); and

Raging with Compassion: Pastoral Responses to the Problem of Evil, by John Swinton (Eerdmans, 2007).

NOTES

National Issues and Tragedies / Natural Disasters

The psalmist declares with confidence: "God is our refuge and strength, a very present help in trouble" (Ps. 46:1). These words have been a comfort to God's people throughout history. Martin Luther's popular hymn *A Mighty Fortress is Our God* is based on Psalm 46. Christians today continue to seek refuge and strength in the One whose presence with us means "we will not fear," not even if "the earth should change [or 'give way'], . . . the mountains shake in the heart of the sea; . . . its waters roar and foam, . . . the mountains tremble with its tumult" (Ps. 46:2–3).

But what if our experience does not match these words, despite our earnest efforts to make them our own? How can we pray when we are less confident, more fearful than we would like to be in the face of real tragedies and inexplicable circumstances that affect millions of people? In an age when wars, famine, natural disasters, and disease persist alongside seemingly daily reports of school shootings, the ravages of addiction, and gross misconduct by our elected officials, what does it look like to come together as a community to seek God on behalf of our communities?

Scripture abounds with examples of God's people turning to God not only during times of personal distress (e.g., 2 Sam. 12:16–17; Jas. 5:14–15), but also to express the needs of a whole nation or society (e.g., Exod. 2:23–25; 1 Sam. 12:10–11; 1 Tim. 2:1–2). In times of national issues and tragedy, including natural disasters, God's word invites us to consider how our prayers together might be characterized by honesty, humility, and hope.

Psalms of individual and corporate lament invite groups to approach God with honesty by naming the truth of tragedy, including the difficult questions it might raise for one's view of God and God's goodness. In the preface to his 1557 commentary on Psalms, the Reformer John Calvin called the book "An Anatomy of all the Parts of the Soul," for it expresses the full range of human emotions: "the Holy Spirit has here drawn to life all the griefs, sorrows, fears, doubts, hopes, cares, perplexities, in short, all the distracting emotions with which the minds of men are wont to be agitated."[27] More than a mirror, the psalms of the Bible are also, according to Calvin, an invitation to approach God as the psalmists did—namely, by taking less care with our words and leaving nothing unsaid. The authors of Psalm 44, for example, attribute their nation's desolation and abandonment to God. Unable to comprehend, much less accept, God's reasons for their

---

[27] John Calvin, *Commentary on Psalms*, Vol. 1 (trans. James Anderson; CreateSpace, 2015), 27.

plight, they call on God to wake up: "Rouse yourself!" (Ps. 44:23). Such raw emotion can be jarring, its vulnerability unsettling. Yet Scripture invites us to leave off sugar coated and guarded speech in the face of adversity. This approach can be a great comfort for groups in prayer by both uniting individuals in the solidarity of shared experience and giving voice to the depth of pain that often marks our common journey.

Such truthfulness in prayer also fosters humility in the face of diverse, frequently complex responses to national issues and tragedies. Not everyone engages adversity in the same way, even when affected by similar circumstances. Jesus warned his followers against seeking explanations for tragedies by speculating about God's judgment against the sins of others (Luke 13:1–5). The proliferation of inflammatory religious rhetoric in national discourses shows how quickly speech becomes a weapon to demean and destroy other people with little thought and even less justification. Christians should take care that such patterns of division do not infect our prayers and thus distort our view of ourselves and God, so that prayer becomes a means of self-elevation at the expense of others rather than serving as a means to seek the Lord, whose grace we all need.

Honesty and humility in prayer challenge our demands for certainty by opening our hearts to the reality that tragic events afflicting an entire nation can arise from complicated causes perhaps decades, even centuries in the making—causes that cannot be reduced to the decisions of a single person or group. In many cases, such as the devastation resulting from natural disasters (earthquakes, hurricanes, tsunamis, volcanic eruptions, etc.), tragedy defies tidy explanations, including all claims regarding human responsibility. Prayer in these instances might focus on lament over the loss of life and livelihood. We might also offer petitions for comfort for those experiencing grief or displacement, wisdom for those charged with providing relief, and the manifold grace of God to meet people struggling in a variety of ways.

Finally, in prayer we should remember that the One to whom we turn is the One in whom we hope. Expectation is the posture of prayer. When faced with concerns that stretch our capacities to comprehend them, not to mention our ability to control them, we rejoice that we are not alone. We gather with others who share our situation. God is in our midst. God hears and acts on our behalf. Although we lack the answers we seek and struggle with the ones we have, in Christ we are assured that God remains with us and for us:

If God is for us, who is against us? He who did not withhold his own Son, but gave him up for all of us, will he not with him also give us everything else? . . . Who will separate us from the love of Christ? Will hardship, or distress, or persecution, or famine, or nakedness, or peril, or sword? . . . No, in all these things we are more than conquerors through him who loved us. For I am convinced that neither death, nor life, nor angels, nor rulers, nor things present, nor things to come, nor powers, nor height, nor depth, nor anything else in all creation, will be able to separate us from the love of God in Christ Jesus our Lord (Rom. 8:32, 35, 37–38).

A prayer such as the following one may bring comfort to people struggling with experiences that are difficult, perhaps impossible to understand and in most cases beyond our control:

In these uncertain and tumultuous times, have mercy on us, O Lord! Be our refuge and strength, a very present comfort and help in trouble. We cry out on behalf of the afflicted. Draw near to those who mourn. Help us to love others well, to listen patiently, and to serve courageously with wise words and just deeds. Give us abundant grace to reach across the divisions that have fractured our communities and nation—discord now magnified in the face of adversity—that we may live in peace with others because of our hope in Christ, through whom you are reconciling the world to yourself and making all things new. Amen.

The Rev. Dr. Kenneth J. Woo
Assistant Professor of Church History

Helpful resources for further reading include:

>   *If God is Good: Faith in the Midst of Suffering and Evil*, by Randy Alcorn (Multnomah, 2014);

>   *The Problem of Pain*, by C. S. Lewis (rev. ed.; HarperOne, 2015); and

>   *Raging with Compassion: Pastoral Responses to the Problem of Evil*, by John Swinton (Eerdmans, 2007).

NOTES

OPPRESSION

Historically, one of the great strengths of African-American Christianity has been the conviction that God is proximate, accessible, and responsive—especially in times of urgent need. In the midst of the bruising oppression of slavery and other forms of systematized injustice and inequality, African-American Christians frequently embraced a conception of God as "refuge and strength, a very present help in trouble" (Ps. 46:1). When doors were closed and avenues cut off, God was viewed as the One capable of "making a way out of no way."[28] When facing opposition and oppression, God was seen as the people's "salvation" and source of courage, the One who "takes me up" when forsaken by all others, and the One who causes their enemies and foes to "stumble and fall" (Ps. 27:1, 2, and 10).

These understandings of God contributed to an African-American social and spiritual agency that encouraged social purposefulness and resourcefulness operating closely together with spiritual confidence and centeredness. Integrations of these social and spiritual postures achieved public expression in the preaching and prayers of African-American Christians—with those dimensions sometimes fueling and giving rise to collective public engagement and activism. More attention has been given to connections between preaching and public activism than to prayer and public activism, but in notable instances prayer has been a central ingredient (if not a precondition) in African-American activism.

Historian Dennis Dickerson draws attention, for example, to a widely supported National Deliverance Day of Prayer spearheaded early in the Civil Rights Movement by two prominent black clergy activists, Adam Clayton Powell Jr. and Archibald J. Carey Jr. The emphasis on prayer in this instance intended a twofold purpose: "deliverance of [activists] in Montgomery and all Americans who are the victims of prejudice" and "salvation for all those whose souls are afflicted with the sin and disease of hatred."[29] An emphasis on prayer was discernible throughout the Civil Rights Movement, with protest marches and actions often being preceded by public prayer and worship services.

---

[28] An African American folk saying declares, "Our God can make a way out of no way . . . . He can do anything but fail." See, for example, *A Way out of No Way: Claiming Family and Freedom in the New South*, by Dianne Swann-Wright (University of Virginia Press, 2002).

[29] Dennis C. Dickerson, *African American Preachers and Politics: The Careys of Chicago* (University Press of Mississippi, 2010), 163.

Although connections between prayer and social justice are certainly not confined to the African-American experience, what historical accounts of the role of prayer during the Civil Rights Movement reinforce is the importance of collective, targeted prayer. Similarly to Jesus' followers, who with singularity of purpose gathered in prayer in the Upper Room following Jesus' ascension (Acts 1:14), activists during the Civil Rights Movement often gathered in churches with a singularity of purpose. What was desired by those gathered in the Upper Room was God's manifestation through the Holy Spirit's presence and anointing. What was desired in countless church gatherings during the Civil Rights Movement was God's manifestation through an empowerment of efforts to bring about an end to formalized racial segregation. In both instances, Christians engaging collectively in purposeful prayer received what they prayed for in the form, one might say, of tongues of fire, hearts on fire, and anointed witness and action.

Engaging collectively in purposeful prayer (including about such matters as oppression and social justice) can position us where a key biblical principle related to prayer can be demonstrated. Jesus said to his disciples, "if two of you agree on earth about anything you ask, it will be done for you by my Father in heaven" (Matt. 18:19). Followers of Jesus in the Upper Room appear to have believed that statement. Followers of Jesus in quite a few Civil Rights Movement prayer services appeared to have believed it. Hopefully today, more of us, desiring manifestations of God's liberating power in our contexts and circumstances, will take that promise to heart as well.

The prayer below expresses our petition and hope in God that oppression will not have the last word:

O God, in times of trouble we have called upon you, and you have answered. When confronted by strong forces, you have empowered us by your Spirit. So in the face of that which oppresses, help us to stand fast in the assurance that we have come this far by faith and by the knowledge that you have never left us or forsaken us. In Christ's name we pray. Amen.

The Rev. Dr. R. Drew Smith
Professor of Urban Ministry

Helpful resources for further consultation include:

An *African Prayer Book*, by Desmond Tutu (Doubleday, 2006);

Meditations of the Heart, by Howard Thurman (Beacon, 1999);

Tears We Cannot Stop: A Sermon to White America (esp. chap. 3), by Michael Eric Dyson (St. Martin's, 2017); and

When Prayer Makes News: Churches and Apartheid, by Allan A. Boesak and Charles Villa-Vicencio (Westminster John Knox, 1986).

NOTES

PERSECUTION (OF THE CHURCH)

Writing to a minority Church perched precariously between competing interests in the Roman Empire, James envisions a connection between testing and maturity: "you know that the testing of your faith produces endurance; and let endurance have its full effect, so that you may be mature and complete, lacking in nothing" (Jas. 1:3–4). I was reminded of this text on a visit to Egypt, where brothers and sisters in Christ exuded resurrection hope while sharing stories of religious persecution and threats of violence. Living as religious minorities through two revolutions has a way of clarifying the nature of Christian identity and discipleship. I met countless Egyptian Christians who testified to the surprising power of the cross to equip and enable the Church for non-violent, loving, and subversive responses to church bombings, social intimidation, and labyrinthine legal challenges to local churches. By the grace of God, their perseverance gives way to hope.

Prayer for the persecuted Church is both simple and confusing. We have a long tradition of celebrating the stoic faithfulness of famous Christian martyrs, while also minimizing the horrors of religious violence with triumphal rhetoric, such as "the blood of the martyrs is the seed of the Church."[30] On the one hand, this tradition makes perfect sense. The mystery of our faith begins with an awareness of such religious violence, for we remember every week at the communion table that Christ died. Remembering the martyrs and those who have faithfully borne up under persecution helps us attend to the cruciform, upside-down dimensions of our faith. Furthermore, we have inherited a tradition that has curated stories of the Christian faith's surviving, growing, and even thriving against difficult odds.

On the other hand, however, our persecution stories lean into gratuitously heroic caricatures. They do for persecution what Mel Gibson's movie *The Passion of the Christ* does for the crucifixion. Action-hero motifs infect our historical imagination such that the persecuted one becomes a beaten and bloodied conqueror in the name of Christ. In such frameworks, we have little room for Jesus' own cry of dereliction ("My God, my God, why have you forsaken me?" Matt. 27:46) or the stories of persecution that demoralized the Church rather than demonstrated its persistent superiority—stories such as the Japanese persecution fictionalized in Shusaku Endo's novel *Silence*.[31]

---

[30] Tertullian, *Apologeticus*, chap. 50.
[31] Translation edition by Picador Modern Classics (2016).

The truth is that "the persecuted Church" has never been a singular or simple construct. We often inflate stories of persecution in the early Church (when Roman persecution was almost always regional and sporadic) while ignoring the systemic brutality inflicted upon Christian groups in the modern era (today for example, the plight of Christian communities across the Middle East). Furthermore, it can be difficult to parse out the differences between ethnic and religious violence in contested regions of the globe. A Christian organization might claim religious persecution, whereas the U.S. State Department understands violence or exclusion as a recent manifestation of ethnic or cultural rivalry. What looks like persecution may be better understood as the consequence of failing political institutions and diminishing social trust.

So how do we pray with and for the persecuted Church? The Bible provides for us at least three different modes of prayer with our persecuted brothers and sisters, and all three merit consideration and practice. First, psalms of lament, such as Psalms 89 and 94, help us wrestle with injustice in the world and teach us to tell the truth about both God and the world. God indeed rules the world, yet justice and righteousness seem like distant promises. These psalms teach us to cry "How long, O LORD?" They emerge from Israel's own exilic experience, and they are prayers we pray with people suffering persecution. Second, we pray with Jesus to "Our Father in heaven" for God's kingdom to come and God's will to be done on earth as it is in heaven (Matt. 6:9). The "How long?" of the psalms becomes concrete as we prayerfully imagine God's reign breaking into the violence of our world.

To pray for God's reign to come in the broken places of our world, however, we need both a theological imagination and an informed opinion. Karl Barth famously encouraged Christians to read the Bible and the newspaper. Perhaps we should also pray through the newspaper for God's reign.

Finally, the Apostle Paul teaches that we fulfill the law of Christ when we bear one another's burdens (Gal. 6:2). Prayer for the persecuted Church becomes most concrete when we pray in partnership with brothers and sisters around the world. Through the near-miraculous connectivity of social media, we can remain in contact with Christians we have met in our travels or through different church ministries. Let us not only keep these brothers and sisters in prayer—let us also remain connected to them and share in their hopes, prayers, and concerns.

And let all of us pray for the persecuted Church around the world:

Heavenly Father, with our sisters and brothers suffering under oppression, violence, stress, and exclusion, we cry out, "How long, O Lord?" How long will corrupt government officials and so-called religious leaders use religious symbols and practices to enrich themselves at the expense of others? How long will failed political and economic institutions leave minority communities vulnerable to ridicule, physical harm, and religious persecution? How long will your people suffer?

Our Father, in whom we "live and move and have our being,"[32] we confess that you are sovereign over all the earth, that while the "kings of the earth take their stand . . . against the Lord,"[33] you will not be moved. We pray, Lord, that your Kingdom come, your will be done on earth as it is in heaven. We pray specifically today for _____ (name of a country, region, or people to focus on for prayer) and for your Church in this place: may they be granted not only perseverance but also hope. May their lives together bear witness to the hope found in the resurrected Jesus Christ.

Finally, Lord, we pray for _____ (names of people you know in this region). May you grant them what they need for today, as well as hope for tomorrow. Bind our hearts to them through your Spirit. In the hope of Jesus Christ our Lord we pray. Amen.

Dr. Scott J. Hagley
Assistant Professor of Missiology

Helpful resources for further consultation include:

> *Beyond Christendom*, by Jehu Hanciles (Orbis, 2008)
> (for understanding the dynamics leading to widespread
> migration);
>
> "Fractured Lands: How the Arab World Came Apart,"
> by Scott Anderson (*NYTimes Magazine*, Aug. 11, 2016;
> see https://www.nytimes.com/interactive/2016/08/11/
> magazine/isis-middle-east-arab-spring-fractured-lands.
> html) (for understanding religious and political tensions in
> the Middle East); and

---

[32] Acts 17:28.
[33] Acts 4:26.

The Tenth Parallel: Dispatches from the Frontline Between Christianity and Islam, by Eliza Griswold (Picador, 2011) (for understanding the sources and realities of interreligious violence and conflict across Africa and Asia).

Notes

Personal Tragedy

Throughout the Bible, we read personal pleas by both those who find themselves in great danger, anguish, or bereavement and those who intercede on behalf of others in such circumstances. These prayers cover a host of distressing situations relating to personal or communal heartbreak and tragedy: Elisha prayed for the Shunammite woman's dead son (2 Kings 4:33); Jairus pled for his daughter (Luke 8:41); Jesus addressed the Father outside Lazarus' tomb (John 11:41–42); Peter prayed for Tabitha (Acts 9:40); Hezekiah petitioned God for health (2 Kings 20:2); Daniel prayed under intense religious persecution (Dan. 6:10, 9:3–4); Jonah prayed from the belly of the great fish (Jonah 2:1) and later when consumed with anger and confusion in Nineveh (4:2); Stephen prayed while being stoned to death (Acts 7:59); Paul prayed when shipwrecked near Malta (Acts 27:29) and later when bitten by a poisonous viper (Acts 28:3); and, of course, Jesus prayed in Gethsemane on the night of his arrest (Matt. 26; Mark 14; Luke 22).

In his teaching Jesus tells us how to pray: "Pray then this way: 'Our Father in heaven . . .'" (Matt. 6:9; cf. Luke 11:2). "Our" reminds us that we are not alone; we are part of a community of believers who can assist us through times of great distress or personal tragedy. In such times, God comforts both the bereaved and the companion seeking to help the griever. Psalm 54:4 may be translated, "God is my helper; the Lord is with those who support/sustain my life."

Jesus' guidance to his disciples also captures both the personal, intimate, present, caring nature of a creator God who walks with us and deals with us as a kinsperson might ("Our Father"; cf. Genesis 2–3) and the power of a transcendent, cosmic God ("in heaven") who brings order from chaos by speaking through majestic, divine fiat (Genesis 1). In times of personal tragedy and direst need, we crave the former, intimate God. But in the very depths of despair, before any healing has begun, the inclination to fear that God is too transcendent to notice us may become all too real.

Sometimes when we pray in our most broken moments, we may perceive no answer, receive no comfort. God seems distant, and we simply cannot understand or explain what has happened. We almost become afraid to pray, or see no point to praying. Our loss is already too real. In these times of feeling helpless, we can encourage others and ourselves to remember that it was the transcendent God of Genesis 1 who hovered over chaos and brought order out of it. God has that desire. God's transcendence can be for us an emblem of his power, not his distance from us.

In times of personal tragedy, praying implies belief that God can and will give comfort and support. Even if our heartache is so great that we cannot immediately make sense of the situation or experience God's response, the act of prayer can serve to focus us on God, thereby stabilizing us. In biblical Hebrew, the verb "to pray" belongs to a class of words that often denotes reflexive action: the benefits of the action return to the doer. By requiring us to center ourselves in God's mercies, prayer helps us "learn" both about ourselves and about God—activities we moderns tend to separate. The Bible does not.

This is not to say, however, that in the immediate, heartbreaking moments of personal tragedy praying is easy, that we feel like doing it, or that we even know what to say should we want to pray. In the deepest depths, personal anguish may become so great that we cannot even speak. But even in our utter weakness and inability to offer so much as a helpless groan, we are not alone; there, the Great Comforter will intercede for us "with sighs too deep for words" (Rom. 8:26).

People caught in the throes of personal tragedy simply need comfort and compassion, not a theology lesson. During the initial shock, the anguished one may be experiencing multiple and possibly conflicting, uncontrollable emotions: painful nostalgia, anger, denial, disbelief, remorse or regret, guilt, even a loss of faith in God. In those awful early moments and days, it is anything but comforting to hear platitudes such as "It was God's will, part of God's plan," "You must accept it and move on," or "All things work together for good." Better to admit there are no clear answers to explain the tragedy. Better simply to reassure the anguished person of God presence. In the case of a loved one who has died, it is a comforting ministry to the survivor(s) to remember the deceased person(s) verbally with honor and love. Often merely our silent presence with and holding the hand of the bereaved communicate the clearest, most needed message.

In ministering to those experiencing personal tragedy, there is perhaps no better collection of writings to guide us than the Psalter. It contains more laments of those in dire distress than any other literary genre. The Psalms address situations of sickness and disease, death, persecution, loneliness and affliction, sinfulness, forsakenness, shame, grief and sorrow, failure of friendship, moral and spiritual weakness, and more. Biblical laments typically include a clear expression of hope (e.g., Ps. 22:9–11), as the psalmists face these tragic circumstances with both heart-rending pleas and beautiful promises of God's presence and love. Even when the severity of illness shakes one's faith, when a person is faced with being "a mere breath," "a sojourner," "a passing guest" in this earthly life, that person can still ask the Lord to listen and not to remain silent before his or her tears (Psalms 39, 41, and 42).

Not long ago, when someone very dear to me lay in the balance between life and death, the Psalms spoke to us as nothing and no one else could do. Psalms 91 and 121 were particularly helpful. God will cover you with his pinions; he will not slumber; he will watch over your life. As I read from the Psalter to comfort my loved one, I suddenly realized how much I myself needed to hear those words. In my feeble attempt to bring comfort to someone else, I found it myself. In those moments, the prayerful psalms were not reduced to academic discussion in the classroom; they became living voices speaking to our very real and near-tragic circumstance. So when we are overcome, distraught, oppressed, anguished, or feel as though we simply want to fly away to a restful place (Psalm 55), we can take refuge in the shadow of God's wings as he fulfills his purpose for us (Pss. 57:1–2; 91:4).

Psalm 77 can also be instructive in anguished circumstances. Ironically, the writer does not specify the nature of his personal tragedy or indicate that deliverance ever came. But whatever the matter, the poet was clearly suffering through a personal tragedy. One could not offer a bleaker, more desperate description of the situation than that found in verses 1–10. The sufferer came to feel that God had forgotten him, perhaps abandoned or even spurned him. The one thread that helped him through the horrifying night of personal anguish was a memory of God's past great deeds (vv. 5–6, 11–12)—even those performed in behalf of others. The supplicant concluded his prayer by quoting an ancient hymn of praise extoling God's power to help and care for his people (vv. 16–20).

Sometimes we can only climb up into our watch tower, wait, and be long-suffering in our prayers (Habakkuk 1–2). As we struggle through the various stages that attend personal tragedy, wait for healing that seems too slow in coming, or experience what feels like unending minutes in which we lack the strength to recognize God's presence and great love for us, we can with God's help follow the psalmists' inclination to recall God's past goodness. As the Holy Spirit intercedes for us when we cannot manage even an utterance, the Psalms have the power to speak *for* us as well as *to* us.

A succinct but meaningful prayer in times of deep anguish comes from Psalm 57:1–3:

Be merciful to me, O God, be merciful to me,
for in you my soul takes refuge;
in the shadow of your wings I will take refuge,
until the destroying storms pass by.
I cry to God Most High,
to God who fulfills his purpose for me.
(May) he send from heaven and save me . . .
. . . (May) God send forth his steadfast love and his faithfulness.

Dr. Ron E. Tappy
G. Albert Shoemaker Professor of Bible and Archaeology and
Project Director of The Zeitah Excavations

Helpful resources for further consultation include:

> *A Grief Observed*, by C. S. Lewis (Harper, 2009);
>
> *Lament for a Son*, by Nicholas Wolterstorff (Eerdmans, 1987);
>
> *Life Together: A Discussion of Christian Fellowship*, by Dietrich Bonhoeffer (Harper and Row, 1954);
>
> *Out of the Depths: The Psalms Speak for Us Today,* by Bernhard W. Anderson (rev. and exp. ed.; Westminster John Knox, 2000); and
>
> *The Theology of Prayer: A Systematic Study of the Biblical Teaching on Prayer*, by Wayne A. Spear (Baker, 1979).

NOTES

PREGNANCY ISSUES

New life enters the world each minute through a pregnant woman's giving birth. The advent is momentous and miraculous. The Lord, the Giver of life, allows women this incredible opportunity of experiencing the forming of another person within their body. But that experience is not universal for women, nor is it easy or without great pain. Many mothers, even most of them will remind us that the pain of childbirth is a mere memory compared to the great joy brought by seeing their newborn children—but the next few paragraphs acknowledge and honor the pain of pregnancy.

Our biology reminds us of the possibility of pregnancy. Each month, from the time of puberty, women are reminded whether they are pregnant or fertile. Birth control does not completely quiet this wondering until menopause ends the possibility of pregnancy. For women trying to get pregnant, this cessation is a painful reminder. For those who are not trying, it often brings a sigh of relief. But all women of childbearing "age and stage" are dealing with this possibility, or the lack of it, in some form or another.

The moment a woman realizes she is pregnant, her life changes. For the rest of her life, this change will be documented in her physical records. Whether or not the pregnancy is planned, wanted, or results in the live birth of a child, the pregnancy is now a part of her physical story. Emotionally and spiritually, how each woman deals with and processes pregnancy and pregnancy loss is different. Those differences need to be respected and honored.

Outside their OB/GYN office, few women discuss their pregnancies that have not resulted in the birth of a live child, but many women have those stories. They are shared carefully when these women discover that others have similar stories of loss. And as these stories escape women's mouths, the pain is real and alive and difficult, no matter how many years have passed.

In such cases, the role of a pastor or lay leader is to give women and their partners the space to talk about these moments in their lives—moments that have caused them some of their greatest pain. If you are let into these family secrets, cherish this confiding in you, and let the family lead you in how to care for them. As in all pastoral care situations, your role is not to fix the problem but to walk with the persons struggling and point them to Jesus. The most valuable things you can offer a woman or couple in the midst of loss surrounding pregnancy are the relationship and hope found in Jesus Christ.

Oftentimes, meaning no harm, pastors, family members, and friends ask questions of women and couples who are in the midst of many pregnancy and fertility issues—questions that are extremely painful. These questions are typically asked rather flippantly and without room for a couple or individual actually to answer them. If you ask such questions in the midst of a long conversation, or within the appropriate context of a conversation in which you sincerely want to hear the answer and have the opportunity to do so, ask them—with sensitivity. But be aware that most blunders occur because the question is asked in a conversation and context that allows inadequate or even no space for an honest response.

Issues surrounding pregnancy usher both great joy and great pain. Below are a few tips for avoiding unfortunate verbal mistakes commonly and frequently made by pastors, lay leaders, and well-meaning friends and family:

1. Do not ask a couple why they don't have children *or* when they are going to have children. Instead, tell them that you believe they would make great parents and that, no matter whether they have children or not, you love and support them.

2. Do not ask a couple who has one child why they have not had more children *or* when they are going to have more children. Instead, tell them they are great parents and that you are very blessed to know their child.

3. Do not ask a woman why she hasn't had children. Do not ask her if she *wants* to have children. This goes for all women of all ages! Instead, affirm her and let her know she is cared for and valued.

Sharing stories of infertility from the Bible can offer important comfort and encouragement to those struggling with this reality in their lives. Some of these stories have a happy ending, some do not. But the longing of these mothers for children rings true for many women still today: Sarah, in Genesis 16–18:18; 21:1–8; the wife and female servants of Abimelech, in Genesis 20; Rebekah, in Genesis 25:19–26; Rachel, in Genesis 30:1–24; the wife of Manoah, in Judges 13; Hannah, in 1 Samuel 1–2:11; Michal, in 2 Samuel 6:23; the Shunammite woman, in 2 Kings 4:8–17; and Elizabeth, in Luke 1:5–25.

The prayer below helps honor both the pain of pregnancy and the pain of infertility.

Lord Jesus, today we lift up to you _____ (name) and _____ (name), who are struggling with the reality of _____ (infertility and/or loss). Lord, we thank you for the deep desire you have placed in their hearts for a child. And Lord, like the weeping of Hannah to Eli, we weep with them. We cry out to you and ask for your mercy. We pray that you would give them comfort, peace, and trust that Jesus loves them no matter what. We commit as a prayerful people to pray continuously for them as they go through this journey and to lift them up in every way we can. In Jesus' name we pray. Amen.

The Rev. Erin M. Davenport, MSW-LSW, '05
Director of the Miller Summer Youth Institute

Helpful resources for further consultation include:

> *Disappointment With God: Three Questions No One Asks Aloud*, by Philip Yancey (Zondervan, 1997);
>
> *I Will Carry You: The Sacred Dance of Grief and Joy*, by Angie Smith (B&H Books, 2010); and
>
> *Without Child: A Compassionate Look at Infertility*, by Martha G. Stout (Harold Shaw, 1990).

NOTES

Prejudice

At the heart of our Christian faith is the conviction that all people are made in the image of God—and so are created good. All people—of all races, ethnicities, languages, and nationalities; all gender identities and sexual orientations; all religions; all body types and hair colors; all abilities; all educational levels, incomes, and classes. All people are made in the good image and likeness of God.

And yet . . . how often we determine, sometimes unconsciously, that one group of people is better than another. How often we deem one person worse than another based on her accent, his income, her gender identity, the number of degrees he has, or the color of his or her skin.

Gracious creator God, stay with me today; awaken my consciousness so that I will see you in the face of everyone I meet.

Our prejudices—our feelings and attitudes about groups of people—are not based on reason or even on our own experience. They are prejudgments based at times on stereotypes or on the self-centered belief that the particular group we ourselves belong to is better in every way than any other. Prejudices never take into account the value of individual difference within groups. Sometimes, as we begin to recognize the fundamental sinfulness of prejudice and realize how deeply seated it is within us, how it reaches back to our childhood, we are tempted to deny it or try to explain it away by saying things like, "Well, that's just the way I was raised."

Gracious, forgiving God, stay with me today; remind me that all people are made in your good image.

The Apostle Peter's prejudice was so ingrained that he thought he shouldn't associate with certain people—such as Cornelius, a Gentile. The conversion in Peter's thinking began with a vision that startled and confused him. At noon one day in Joppa, as he was waiting for lunch to be prepared, he fell asleep and dreamed, as might be expected, about food. He saw a great sheet filled with all kinds of animals, including birds and reptiles, and heard a voice saying something along the lines of, "Here's lunch; help yourself." Peter responded, "No, I would never eat such things; they are unclean." Then visitors arrived and invited him to travel with them to Caesarea to meet Cornelius. When they arrived, Peter began by saying that he should not even be talking with his hosts—but then, in a sign of his own conversion, he said, "God has shown me that I should not call anyone profane or unclean" (Acts 10:28). Hear the echo of that statement in Romans 2:11, where Paul writes, "For God shows no partiality."

In fact, the theme that all people are acceptable to God and that we should not show prejudice against anyone runs throughout Scripture—as seen most profoundly in the way that Jesus accepted everyone, especially those found unacceptable by others.

Gracious God of all, stay with me today; grant me the grace and courage to follow Jesus and his example of finding everyone acceptable.

For some of us, the prejudice of others means that we live in constant oppression and so find it difficult to remember that we, too, are made in the wonderful likeness of God.

Gracious creator God, stay with me today; restore in me the joy that comes from knowing that I am made in your image.

The following prayer, written by J. Philip Newell, speaks to me. I pray that it speaks renewal and restoration to you and to those with and for whom you pray for healing from prejudice, whether harbored or suffered.

In your light, Gracious God,
May we glimpse again your image deep within us
the threads of eternal glory
woven into the fabric of every man and woman.
Again may we catch sight of the mystery of the human soul
fashioned in your likeness
deeper than knowing
more enduring than time.
And in glimpsing these threads of light
Amidst the weakness and distortions of my life
Let me be recalled
To the strength and beauty deep in my soul.
Let us be recalled
To the strength and beauty of your image
in every living soul.

The Rev. Dr. David Esterline
President and Professor of Cross-cultural Theological Education

Helpful resources for further consultation include:

Celtic Benediction: Morning and Night Prayer, by J. Philip Newell (Eerdmans, 2000).

NOTES

Relationships Strained and Broken

In Genesis 2:18 we read that God, after creating the first human being, decided it was "not good that the man should be alone"—so God created another person. This part of the creation story reminds us that, from the beginning, we were created to be in relationship with others. Human relationships are the source of some of life's greatest joys. After all, it is in relationship that we learn to love and care for others, and to receive love and care in return. For this reason, relationships can also be the source of some of our deepest pain. Strained or broken relationships may create wounds that are very difficult to heal.

Often when people are experiencing these kinds of struggles in their relationships, they reach out for support from their community of faith. Praying with someone in this circumstance can, in itself, be a way to accompany the person on a path toward healing. Even so, it is important to be sensitive to the many complex circumstances that may be involved. It may not always be possible to know all the details of what has happened in a relationship. In fact, it is likely that you will only know the story from the perspective of the person who has requested prayer.

In this situation, it is not the responsibility of the one ministering to try to sort out the "facts" of what happened; rather, the minister's main task is to listen carefully to what the person shares and to help name the pain, grief, and other emotions the sufferer is experiencing. Helping someone acknowledge the feelings that result from strained or broken relationships is an important step, because this acknowledgment may give the person permission to be more honest with God in prayer. Allowing individuals to express their pain and grief is especially important if the possibility exists that the relationship in question cannot be mended. Here, the Psalms may be particularly helpful as a resource for prayer since they express such a wide range of human emotions. Consider Psalms 4, 27, 40, 42, 91, and 103 when praying with people who are struggling with strained or broken relationships.

When you pray with someone who is lamenting a damaged relationship, it is also important to ensure that you are not giving relational advice or encouraging false hope. As noted above, you will likely only know one person's perspective on the situation, so it is vital to remember that your role is to offer support and prayer—and not attempt to tell the person what he or she should do in the relationship. If you sense that someone wants specific relationship advice, consider referring her or him to a professional counselor or therapist who specializes in this kind of work. Also, avoid making comments such as "I'm sure everything will be fine" and "I know that God will make this situation right." We cannot know the future, and we cannot make promises about how others will respond to a person or about how God may be working in a particular situation. Making these kinds of statements may relieve our own anxiety in the moment, but doing so risks planting false hope in someone who is already vulnerable.

Perhaps the most important ministry you can offer if you are called upon to pray with someone experiencing a strained or broken relationship is simply to be present—to listen carefully without giving advice or trying to "fix" the person's situation. Reassure the individual that God has promised to be with us throughout all the trials we experience in life, and that God can hold all the anger, sadness, and fear we may need to express through prayer. Remind yourself that it is not your job to heal another person; God is the One who leads us all toward healing and restoration. Simply by offering support and expressing care, you can serve as a powerful reminder of God's healing presence, even in the midst of struggle and pain.

A prayer such as the one below may be helpful as you minister to someone in this circumstance:

Gracious God, we thank you today for the gift of being in relationship with one another. We give you thanks especially for all the people who love and care for _____ (name/names). We ask that you would help _____ (name/names) to feel your love today and to know that you have created him/her/them as your beloved child(ren). As _____ (name/names) goes through this very challenging time, help him/her/them to sense your presence and to trust that you are guiding him/her/them toward healing. We ask that you would grant faith, hope, and peace to _____ (name/names) for this day and for the days to come. Amen.

The Rev. Dr. Leanna K. Fuller
Associate Professor of Pastoral Care

Helpful resources for further consultation include:

> *Cultivating Wholeness: A Guide to Care and Counseling in Faith Communities*, by Margaret Zipse Kornfeld (Continuum, 2000);
>
> *Listening and Caring Skills: A Guide for Groups and Leaders*, by John Savage (Abingdon, 1996); and

Pray without Ceasing: Revitalizing Pastoral Care, by Deborah van Deusen Hunsinger (Eerdmans, 2006).

NOTES

Sin

One of the most influential theologians of prayer was the early church father Origen. Born in Egypt, probably in Alexandria, in 185 AD, Origen was distinguished from an early age by a single-minded desire to know and serve God. He became known as "the man of steel" because of his extraordinary ascetical feats: walking barefoot, fasting, limiting his sleep, and renouncing his sexual desires. But for Origen, self-limitation was not a way to punish himself for sin but rather a way to open up space to think and pray about divine things.

"Divine things." In his famous treatise *On Prayer*, Origen argues that the most important thing for which we can pray is to contemplate God and to enter into his life. The matters that ordinarily constitute the petitions of our prayers—worries about health, relationships, and worldly success—pull us away from God. When we pray for self-defined needs and wants, we are actually praying to ourselves, rather than to God.

Instead, says Origen, let us pray that "the kingdom of God . . . spring up in [us], bear fruit, and be rightly perfected." Let us "peer beyond the created order, . . . gaze at the glory of the Lord with unveiled face, . . . [and] partake of the divine and intelligible radiance." Origen goes so far as to ask that we be "nourished by God the Word, who was in the beginning with God, . . . [so that] we may be made divine."

For Christians today, all this may seem like sheer spiritual escapism when what is needed, we believe, are prayers and interventions for a world that is all too broken and hurting. Rather than looking for a world beyond, we think that we should call on God to give us the strength to make this world—the one before our very eyes—better. In Lord's Day worship, pastors lift up—perhaps by name—people who are struggling with cancer, grieving a loss, or longing for direction in life. We pray for justice and peace: "Thy kingdom come, thy will be done, on earth as it is in heaven."

But Origen is convinced that if we pray for heavenly things, God will provide for our mortal bodies as well. And if we draw closer to God, God will teach us that whatever earthly blessings we receive are but a foretaste of the more amazing spiritual blessings that he offers to us. Health and strength and daily bread—or their absence—can point us to a deeper, more enduring life, a life of trust in, and gratitude and praise for, the God to whom we belong in life and in death.

Origen himself would be martyred for his faith in 253. But he believed that "if all . . . [is] put in harmony by the Word of God . . . bodily sufferings [are] nothing but an insignificant scratch, indeed less than a scratch."

Consider offering this simple prayer with and for a person struggling with sin:

O Lord, teach us again how to pray—not only for the things of this world, but also to contemplate your holy mystery that has come close to us in Jesus Christ. As we receive your blessings in this life, open us to life eternal. We pray in the name of the resurrected Savior. Amen.

The Rev. Dr. John P. Burgess
James Henry Snowden Professor of Systematic Theology

Helpful resources for further consultation include:

> *The Confessions of St. Augustine*, by Saint Augustine of Hippo (multiple publishers);
>
> "How Should Christians Handle Besetting Sins," blog post by R. C. Sproul (June 3, 2016), https://www.ligonier.org/blog/how-should-christians-handle-besetting-sins/;
>
> *The Imitation of Christ*, by Saint Thomas à Kempis (multiple publishers);
>
> *Origen On Prayer*, by Adamantius Origen (Beloved, 2015);
>
> "Sin and Renewing Relationships," pages 51–64 in *Confessing Our Faith: The Book of Confessions for Church Leaders*, by John Burgess (Westminster John Knox, 2018); and
>
> "What I Learned About My Sins at Sixty-Four: How to Make War on Old Enemies," blog post by John Piper (Sept. 11, 2018), https://www.desiringgod.org/articles/what-i-learned-about-my-sins-at-sixty-four.

NOTES

SUICIDE

I am counted among those who go down to the Pit;
I am like those who have no help,
like those forsaken among the dead,
like the slain that lie in the grave,
like those whom you remember no more,
for they are cut off from your hand (Ps. 88:4–5).

These poignant verses express some of the pathos both of persons contemplating suicide and people who have lost a loved one to suicide. It is important to recognize that praying with people contemplating suicide is a distinctly different topic from praying with people grieving loss from suicide. In the former situation, it is essential that the individual involved find help from a qualified and experienced counseling professional, as well as receive spiritual guidance and support. Since most of us are unqualified to assess whether someone is suicidal, it is crucial to learn what questions to ask and what to do if you are at all concerned about someone's safety and need to guide him or her to appropriate assistance. (For help in doing so, see the organizations listed below.)

Individuals grieving the loss of a loved one from suicide often need help from a qualified and experienced counseling professional, too. And they also need spiritual guidance and support. But the call to pray with someone who has suffered such a loss can be terrifying. What does it mean that a beloved friend or family member has seemingly made a choice against life, has taken action in a way that violates the basic human instinct in favor of self-preservation? A parent has died, rather than persevere to care for a child; a child has ended a life that his or her parents and grandparents cherish far more than their own; a sibling has communicated to brothers and sisters that their shared life experience is not worth sustaining. Those who die by suicide do terrible violence to their bodies; they often die alone and in deep psychic pain. The horror of the event is indescribable. The anguish and guilt experienced by those left behind render them inconsolable. How in the world can you pray with someone who feels, every day, that she has been rejected and forsaken by a loved one and, quite possibly, by God as well, or that he has been flung into the endless depths of a dark well of despair?

It can help to learn something about suicide loss before trying to pray with someone who has experienced it firsthand. It can help to know that experts estimate that 90 percent of deaths by suicide are a consequence of undiagnosed and/or untreated mental illness. Excepting those making considered decisions in response to life-diminishing illnesses, people do not "choose" to die, nor do they choose to hurt or damage the people they love. They have not "committed" a crime. People who die by suicide are trying to end intolerable pain.

It can help to know that their loved ones, in addition to being left with the word "Why?" echoing throughout the remainder of their lives, will usually be devastated and immobilized by guilt and shame. They often wonder either why they didn't do more to help the person they have lost, or how it can be that they did not even know the depth of their loved one's pain, and they are horrified to realize that their loved one, the beneficiary of love and support from others, has "thrown it all away." It can help to realize that survivors will bump into the stigma of suicide where they least expect it—a refusal to conduct a funeral, avoidance by acquaintances in the street, intimations that they are to blame. It can help to know they are often angered and hurt by the responses of others.

Praying with someone about loss from suicide is not the time for casual platitudes about God's plan or God's supposed need for another angel in heaven. It is most especially not a time to try to tell a survivor—someone who has lived through a loved one's death by suicide—those often misquoted words, "God never gives us more than we can handle," erroneously based on 1 Corinthians 10:13, which specifically addresses temptation to sin, not endurance of grief. To say in these circumstances that God is implicated in some sort of test of one's capacity for managing traumatic experiences may result in the suicide survivor's further dismay and alienation from God. Neither is it the time to say, "I know how you feel," since (unless you yourself are a survivor) you do *not* know, nor to say, "I can't imagine." The latter comment establishes a barrier between you and someone who already feels isolated from others, and it conveys a sense that what has happened is so awful, you cannot bear to enter into the experience even as a companion.

Prayer with a person experiencing loss from suicide is a time to listen, to sit still, and to be present. It is a time to make space for expressions of rage, of agony, of astonishment, and of rejection of faith. It is a time to make it possible for stories to be told about loved ones now gone. "Tell me what your mother is like." "What is one of your favorite memories?" You might ask someone how he or she imagines the moments after the loved one's death. You do not have to find those ideas compatible with your own or give a lecture about Christian doctrine—your call is to offer the survivor the gift of attentive listening. It can be difficult to remember that companionship and prayer in silence can be much more effective than words, no matter how eloquent, when the unthinkable has happened. A willingness to stay with someone through the wilderness is of far more significance than the most profound speech made in an attempt to lead someone prematurely into a space of healing.

I have asked a number of suicide survivors what they have found most helpful in prayer. Many of them mention the Psalms, as well as fiction and poetry in which sorrow is articulated and assurances of God's boundless love are found. For survivors who are tormented by questions of life after death, books containing reassuring depictions of heaven can be helpful. Psalm 88, the only one of the psalms of lament in which there is no articulation of a turning point toward gratitude and hope, can be deeply meaningful to people who wonder whether any passages in the Bible bear witness to their feelings. (It might be noted that, despite conveying despair, Psalm 88 is addressed to God and reflects a dark confidence that God will hear the psalmist's angry and even sarcastic entreaties.)

Suicide survivors are living the consequences of a loved one's having reached a point beyond what was tolerable, but the loved one's arrival at that destination was not the work of God. The scriptural path for survivors of suicide leads, I believe, toward Romans 8:38–39 and Revelation 21:4—passages well worth sharing with someone who has known this loss, though even these passages may be too much for a survivor to bear at first. When the immediate experience of catastrophe passes, those left behind encounter the crushing realization that their loved one died with a wearying and excruciating sense of emptiness and separation from God, from love—from however their loved one might have characterized "the Holy" in his or her life.

Our hope can be that, someday, the survivor(s) of suicide with whom you are praying will gain confidence in the assurance that, appearances to the contrary, there can be no separation from the love of God—that there will, indeed, be a New Creation in which God will wipe away every tear, and "mourning and crying and pain will be no more" (Rev. 21:4). We cannot force fractured spirits into such a conviction, but we can be present to them in the knowledge that our simple availability will be a prayer in itself.

A possible prayer using words might be as follows:

O God, from whom nothing can ever separate us, my dearest _____ (name of suicide survivor) is in your hands. Surround him/her with the light of your love and with assurances of love and safety. Help him/her to find a way to live again and to know that, even in the most desperate of situations and most disastrous of events, you are there—unseen and unheard, perhaps, but nevertheless present and active in our broken and hurting lives. These requests I make in the name of the One who came that we might live anew. Amen.

The Rev. Mary Robin Craig '10
Pastor, Spiritual Director, and Suicide Prevention/Mental Health Advocate

Helpful resources for further consultation include:

Poetry for prayer:

"After great pain, a formal feeling comes—," by Emily Dickinson, in *The Poems of Emily Dickinson: Reading Edition* (ed. Ralph W. Franklin; The Belknap Press of Harvard University Press, 1998, 1999);

"Love Sorrow," in *Red Bird* (Beacon, 2009), and "Heavy," in *Thirst* (Beacon, 2007), by Mary Oliver; and

"The Wires of the Night," in *Questions about Angels*, by Billy Collins (University of Pittsburgh Press, 1999).

Organizations with help for those who are suicidal and those who have experienced suicide loss:

Action Alliance, http://actionallianceforsuicideprevention. org/faith-communities-task-force;

Alliance of Hope for Suicide Survivors, www. allianceofhope.org;

The American Foundation for Suicide Prevention, www. afsp.org; and

Soul Shop: Ministering to Suicidal Desperation, www. soulshopmovement.org.

NOTES

TEMPTATION

Prayer and temptation are linked in what is, arguably, the most famous and maybe the greatest prayer in the New Testament: The Lord's Prayer (Matt. 6:9–13; Luke 11:2–4). This prayer contains a request that we not be led into temptation. The close link between temptation and prayer reflected in The Lord's Prayer is sustained by other passages in the New Testament. For example, in the Garden of Gethsemane Jesus roused his sleeping disciples with the words, "Keep watching and praying so that you may not enter into temptation," or as the NRSV translates the last phrase, ". . . come into the time of trial" (Matt. 26:41).

The connection between the experiences of prayer and temptation prompts at least two questions: "What is temptation?" and "How does prayer minister to us in times of temptation?"

What is temptation? I suspect that if you were to ask people what comes to mind when they hear the word "temptation," most of them would report thinking of the term in a quasi-religious sense. Don't give in to it. Resist it. Or, as urged increasingly often by advertisers, indulge it! Temptation is the enticement to do something bad, to violate a rule, to disrespect a norm— to do something that is so clearly (though sadly, as some people see it, so deliciously) wrong that "the wrath of God" or some other authority is sure to fall down upon the transgressor. While in some settings that result may come to fruition, such a view of temptation is a very narrow one.

The word temptation in the New Testament—the word that appears in The Lord's Prayer—is the noun *peirasmos*, which basically means "test," whether a period of testing or a process of testing. It occurs 21 times in the New Testament in a total of 26 verses. The corresponding verb, *peirazo*, means to "take a test" or, in its passive voice, "to be tested." That word occurs 38 times in the New Testament in a total of 34 verses. While often bearing religious connotations, then, these words simply refer to taking a test or being tested.

When we think of tests, we normally think of some kind of educational setting, be it academic or vocational, in which we are tested on how much we know or how competent we are with certain skills—what do you know, and what can you do? But these contexts are not the only ones for testing. Life itself is an arena of tests where we face a wide range of decisions about what to do and how to act. These existential tests reveal far more than what we know or what we can do. These "temptation-tests" reveal who we are. And it is in these settings that prayer becomes particularly significant.

How does prayer minister to us in times of temptation? Prayer, in its most authentic form, is making a connection. When we pray in the midst of life and its "tests," we are making a threefold connection through the power of God's grace. As Paul reminds us in Romans 8:26, none of us really knows how to pray, but the Spirit makes possible our connection with the Creator when we use our words, thoughts, and yearnings to reach toward God. In the act of prayer, mediated by the Spirit, we are connected to God—the source of our strength for "passing the test," for not entering into temptation.

And since God is the foundation of all creation, through God we are also connected to others. In prayer, then—both individually regarding our personal temptations and with other people facing tests of their own—we become aware of our responsibility to love others, to seek their good through mercy and justice. We are renewed, inspired, and empowered to be disciples of the risen Christ.

As we pray to experience God's grace and mercy through periods of testing—times of temptation—the close connection maintained with our Creator enables us to be God's disciples—to enter into right relations with God and with other people, to walk faithful paths that honor the Lord Jesus Christ, and to become the persons God has created us—in God's own image—to be.

In praying with someone who is experiencing temptation, who is undergoing a test, consider using language such as that in the prayer below:

Merciful God, in this time of testing, help your child _____ (name) to know the comfort of your presence, the strength of your Spirit, and the assurance of your Son's Lordship as together we seek to do your will. We make these requests in the gracious name of Jesus. Amen.

The Rev. Dr. David L. Morse
Adjunct Professor of Methodist Studies

Helpful resources for further consultation include:

The Greatest Prayer: Rediscovering the Revolutionary
Message of The Lord's Prayer (esp. chap. 8), by John
Dominic Crossan (Harper One, 2010); and

"Temptation," page 494 in Dictionary of Theology, by Karl
Rahner and Herbert Vorgrimler (Crossroad, 1985).

NOTES

Uncertainty About the (Earthly) Future

A spouse says, "I need to talk to you, and you'd better sit down for this." A physician calls with an invitation to come in to discuss your recent medical tests. A manager summons you to her office in the midst of a downsizing at your workplace. Each of these conversations can render suddenly uncertain what you thought was a stable, predictable future. And congregations are filled with people for whom unexpected events and unwelcome news are throwing well-ordered lives into chaos.

But remember also: *Every* earthly future is uncertain. And some spiritual traditions have found ways to embrace the uncertainty of everyday life.

For example, the ancient Celts had a tradition of viewing life as a *perigrinatio*—a journey with no firm destination. They viewed life as a journey of discovery as one walked with God into the unpredictable. Sometimes Celtic Christians would set out on a journey in a small boat called a coracle—a vessel with no rudder, sails, or oars—to travel wherever the waves of the sea and the Spirit of God led.

That image of sailing in a coracle provides a wonderful metaphor for life. Every day, when your feet hit the floor and slide into your slippers, and you shuffle into the kitchen to pour the coffee, you are already in a coracle, the Celtic tradition teaches—on an adventure into an unknown future, however known the journey seems, however well-planned the day. The Celtic notion of life as a journey invites a shift in perspective: each moment becomes a fresh, fathomless mystery, a wave you've never ridden, a surf you've never sailed. A boat never travels the same river twice. Every earthly future is uncertain.

Yes, Christian leaders find themselves praying with people for whom specific events have upended plans, and pastors are first and foremost teachers of prayer. But one of the chief pastoral tasks is to help every person under one's care learn to discover that *all* our futures are uncertain. And then to live life accordingly—abandoned to God in trust. So whether you find yourself ministering to a person who's received a new diagnosis of cancer, or a new retiree with a well-planned next decade, keep in mind the points below as you pray with and instruct that person in the practice of prayer.

Pray to embrace the uncertainty. Uncertainty is not something to run from—in fact, we can't escape it. So we can pray that, in whatever our earthly circumstance, the Spirit of God will help us to loosen our grip on our imagined sense of control and accept the uncertainty of our lives.

Pray for the grace to trust God's loving presence. Only one thing is certain—that God's unfailing, loving presence will never leave us. I cannot imagine anything more important than praying to God to give us the grace to trust God's loving, sustaining presence in each moment—whatever that moment entails.

Pray to learn to receive the present as a gift. Even as we learn to embrace an uncertain earthly future and grow in our trust of God's loving presence, we can also ask God to give us the grace to receive the present moment as a gift. Our futures may be uncertain, but the present is here—often full of beauty and joy and love. But we can miss the present because our fear too often fixates on the future. And even when the present offers pain, sorrow, and tragedy, we can ask to glimpse more clearly the ways God is with us.

Finally, we can *pray to stay faithful on the journey.* Even when facing an uncertain earthly future, we are still called to love as God loves, offer hope when we can, and serve our neighbors. As we walk into the future, we can ask to be given the grace to continue to love others, offer grace, and extend care. We can ask to share God's love with open hearts and generous spirits, whenever the future opens possibilities for such love.

Thomas Merton offers a well-known prayer that begins, "My Lord God, I have no idea where I am going. I do not see the road ahead of me. I cannot know for certain where it will end."[34] That prayer names the condition for each one of us. Some people know this uncertainty acutely—life's events have made clear how dubious the future can be. Others of us, who think our futures are sure, who believe we are in control of how it will end, need to learn the truth of this prayer. Whichever group we are in, we can always pray that God will help us acknowledge and accept the uncertainty of our earthly lives, grow our trust in God's loving presence, receive the gift of life in this moment as a gift of grace, and continue to serve others in love as we ride our little coracles into the unknown, upheld all the while by God's infinite love.

Merton ends his prayer by expressing the trust we might all aspire to as we face the unknown: "Therefore I will trust you always, though I may seem to be lost and in the shadow of death. I will not fear, for you are ever with me, and you will never leave me to face my perils alone."[35]

---

[34] Thomas Merton, *Thoughts in Solitude* (Farrar, Straus and Giroux, 1999), 79.
[35] Merton, *Thoughts in Solitude*, 79.

Gracious God, each day we awaken not knowing what the future will hold. Help us to let go of our need to control the future, so that we might be open to your grace and presence in each moment. When uncertainty causes us to worry, may we know the certainty of your love. And may what we learn as we face the unknown help us to open ourselves in love to others who fear the future. Amen.

The Rev. Dr. L. Roger Owens
Associate Professor of Christian Spirituality and Ministry

Helpful resources for further consultation include:

> *Everything Happens for a Reason (and Other Lies I've Loved)*, by Kate Bowler (Random House, 2018);

> *Julian of Norwich: Selections from Revelations of Divine Love*, annotated by Mary Earle (SkyLight Paths, 2013); and

> *Thoughts in Solitude*, by Thomas Merton (Farrar, Straus and Giroux, 1999).

NOTES

SAMPLE PRAYERS

"Are any among you suffering? They should
pray. Are any cheerful? They should sing
songs of praise. Are any among you sick?
They should call for the elders of the church
and have them pray over them . . . The prayer
of the righteous is powerful and effective."

— James 5:13–14, 16 —

"In everything by prayer and supplication
with thanksgiving let your requests be
made known to God."

— Philippians 4:6 —

ABUSE SUFFERED (PHYSICAL AND EMOTIONAL)

Gracious God, we thank you for your deep, deep love for your whole creation, and for all your people, who are made in your image. This day, we pray especially for your beloved child, _____ (name). Help _____ (name) to sense your tender care, even in the midst of very difficult circumstances. With thanks for your abiding presence we pray. Amen.

ADDICTION AND SUBSTANCE ABUSE

God grant me the serenity to accept the things I cannot change; courage to change the things I can; and wisdom to know the difference. Living one day at a time; enjoying one moment at a time; accepting hardships as the pathway to peace; taking, as He did, this sinful world as it is, not as I would have it; trusting that He will make all things right if I surrender to His Will; that I may be reasonably happy in this life and supremely happy with Him forever in the next. Amen.

ADOPTION

God of life, who graciously adopted us into your family through Jesus Christ, grant open eyes and hearts that we might see the needs of children beyond our own family circles. Give _____ (name/s) wisdom to discern your leading in considering the adoption of a child in need of earthly parents who will make your great love known to him or her. And give us, your adopted children, the courage to redraw family lines so that we, relying on your grace, which is sufficient for the needs of all, might consider each child as our own. In the strong name of Jesus Christ I pray. Amen.

ANGER AND VIOLENCE

O God, so much makes us angry, but so much of our anger is petty. We seethe when someone cuts us off in traffic. We boil inside when we learn someone has spoken ill of us. Redirect our anger toward what really matters. Help us to see the evil in the world and to direct our prayers toward those who suffer from it. Be with all the victims of abuse, those who live in places torn apart by war, and those whose lives are at risk because of disease, famine, and poverty. Let your will be done on earth as it is in heaven. In the name of Jesus we pray. Amen.

ANXIETY

We begin our prayer in the name of God, who gives us life at this very moment;
in the name of Jesus Christ, who embraces our wounds and restores us to wholeness;
in the name of the Holy Spirit, who breathes Christ's gift of peace in us.

(Speak in a calm and steady voice matching the breath of the person:)
I invite you now to
Take in a slow, deep breath;
Notice the breath entering your nose,
Feel the coolness touch the back of the throat,
Feel the rise in your belly, lungs, chest.
Gently, slowly exhale;
Notice your shoulders falling away from your ears,
Descending through your chest, lungs, belly.
Take in another slow deep breath;
Feel the rise in your belly, lungs, and chest as they fill with this life force we call breath,
The breath of the Living God, God's Ruah.
Slowly exhale, allowing the breath of God's life to fill every cell of your being.

(Here one could slowly read Mark 4:35–39,
"On that day, when evening had come, he said to them, 'Let us go across to the other side.' And leaving the crowd behind, they took him with them in the boat, just as he was. Other boats were with him. A great windstorm arose, and the waves beat into the boat, so that the boat was already being swamped. But he was in the stern, asleep on the cushion; and they woke him up and said to him, 'Teacher, do you not care that we are perishing?' He woke up and rebuked the wind, and said to the sea, 'Peace! Be still!' Then the wind ceased, and there was . . . calm," ending with a paraphrase of Jesus' words, *"Quiet now, be calm,"* then continue with the following:)

Take in another slow, deep breath,
Opening to receive the breath of Christ's Spirit,
Filling your chest, lungs, and heart with Christ's peace:
"Peace I leave with you; my peace I give to you" (John 14:27).
Slowly exhale, allowing Christ's peace
To fill every cell of your being.
And for this moment and beyond

There is space in your brain,
And Christ's gift of peace in your heart.
Glory be to God, whose power working in us
Can do infinitely more that we can ask or even imagine (Eph. 3:20);
All glory and praise be to you, O God. Amen.

BEREAVEMENT

Lord Jesus, you wept at the tomb of your friend Lazarus. You know our loss and pain from the inside. Be with your child _____ (name) right now, we pray. Surround her/him with your love, undergird her/him with your peace and strength. Be very real to _____ (name) in these days of grief, Abba, and grant that as she/he is able to hear it, the good news of Christ's resurrection would fill her/him with hope. We pray in the name the One who has "borne our griefs, and carried our sorrows." Amen.

CONFLICT AND CONTROL

Holy God, we thank you that you have created each one of us with unique gifts and callings. When we experience tension or pain because of our differences, grant us compassion for one another. Remind us that even when we disagree, we are united in our identity as your children and in the work to which you have called us. Help us now to discern your will and to follow where you lead—together. Amen.

CRISES

God of mercy and God of grace, the waters of this crisis are becoming overwhelming for _____ (name), who, out of fear of only making things worse, does not trust him/herself to make the right decision at this time. We know that at every turn you are there, but the journey through seems daunting. Hold the hand of _____ (name), Lord, and walk him/her through. May your Spirit serve as _____'s (name) compass, and may _____'s (name) current misfortune and need for your help serve to remind him/her of your trustworthy love and to remind others of your grace.

DEPRESSION

Holy God, who in Jesus Christ comes into our world to be the Light that no darkness can overcome, I pray now in this moment for my friend, _____ (name). You alone know the inner mysteries of our human minds, so often filled with negative thoughts and unrelenting anxiety. Through the healing power of our Savior, Jesus Christ, grant _____ (name) relief from depression and all despair. Give _____ (name) that peace that passes all understanding, through Christ I pray. Amen.

DISABILITY AND PHYSICAL TRAUMA

Christ has no body now but yours. No hands, no feet on earth but yours. Yours are the eyes through which he looks compassion on this world. Yours are the feet with which he walks to do good. Yours are the hands through which he blesses all the world. Yours are the hands, yours are the feet, yours are the eyes, you are his body. Christ has no body now on earth but yours.

— attributed to St. Teresa of Ávila

Loving Creator God, you have made each person in your image, and you invite each person to live in wholeness through relationship with you. Be with us in our doubts and limitations, our gifts and strengths. Heal every one of us from the false assumptions about ourselves and others that divide us, so that we may be unified with each other in our love for you. Amen.

DISCERNMENT

Thanks be to you, my Lord Jesus Christ, for all the benefits you have given me, for all the pains and insults you have borne for me. O most merciful redeemer, friend and brother, may I know you more clearly, love you more dearly, and follow you more nearly, day by day. Amen.

— St. Richard of Chichester

My Lord God, I have no idea where I am going. I do not see the road ahead of me. I cannot know for certain where it will end. Nor do I really know myself, and the fact that I think that I am following your will does not mean that I am actually doing so. But I believe that the desire to please you does in fact please you. And I hope I have that desire in all that I am doing. I hope that I will never do anything apart from that desire. And I know that if I do this you will lead me by the right road, though I may know nothing about it. Therefore will I trust you always, though I may seem to be lost and in the shadow of death. I will not fear, for you are ever with me, and you will never leave me to face my perils alone.

— Thomas Merton

DISCOURAGEMENT

Holy and most loving God, you know our every need, our every hurt, and our every pain. In times when we feel discouraged by the circumstances of life, provide us with strength, guidance, and wisdom. Remind us that you did not call us to be successful but to be faithful and trusting. I pray for my brother/sister _____ (name) and ask that, as he/she deals with _____ (difficulty), he/she is filled with the power of the Holy Spirit and knows the peace that comes only through being a beloved child of God. When words fail _____ (name), give him/her your words that the light of Christ may overcome the darkness and joy fill his/her heart. In the name of our risen and living Lord, Jesus the Christ, I pray. Amen.

DOUBT AND UNCERTAINTY ABOUT FAITH

Lord, we do not know what to pray, and we do not know what to make of you. We are like Jacob on the banks of the Jabbok, on the border of the promised land, looking in from the outside. But like Jacob in that pivotal moment, we will never stop wrestling with you. We cry out to you now from the place of our estrangement. Bring us home, we pray. Amen.

DYING WITHOUT KNOWING GOD

O Heavenly Father, in your Son Jesus Christ you have given to us sure hope and the assurance that you hold every one of your creatures in your care. We pray that you would shed forth upon your whole Church, both in paradise and on earth, the bright beams of your light and heavenly comfort. Help us, we pray, to cast our cares upon you, in the hope that we, with those whom we love, may enter, in the last day, into your eternal glory. Give us faithfulness in prayer and the power to live as people who believe in the communion of saints, the forgiveness of sins, and the resurrection to life everlasting. By your Holy Spirit, strengthen in us this faith and hope all the days of our life, through the love of your Son, Jesus Christ our Savior, who lives and reigns with you, Father, and the Holy Spirit, one God, forever and ever. Amen.

FAMILY PROBLEMS

Gracious God, you know all too well what it is like for your family to face problems. You have seen your sons and daughters struggle with deep pain, fight with one another, fail to fulfill their promises, and even walk away from you. There is no struggle that you do not know intimately, and we are grateful for your care for us.

We are bold to ask, then, Lord, for your presence with us. Forgive our own failures, and help us to forgive those who have failed us. Mend our brokenness, and heal those we love. Help us to receive the love that others offer and not to be ashamed of our need. And, above all, dearest Lord, help us to know deep in our hearts that we are not alone. All these things we pray in the name of our brother and savior, Jesus Christ. Amen.

FINANCIAL DISTRESS

Dear Lord, help _____ (name) to find firm ground in an uncertain economy. As _____ (name) seeks work and assistance, give him/her strength not to be anxious when things seem to be going nowhere. Give _____ (name) patience not to despair when things look bleak; give _____ (name) serenity to know that you are right here, present with him/her, helping to carry his/her cross each day. May _____ (name) do your will in all things that your holy name may be praised! Thank you, Lord, for all the ways that you care for and protect _____ (name). For all things we are truly grateful. Amen.

FORGIVENESS

Lord God, we know that you do not require us to use many words in humbly asking for or offering forgiveness. Please help _____ (name) to be able to say, simply, "I am sorry," both to you and to the person she/ he has wronged. Show _____ (name) how to do better next time. Give her/him the courage to make this situation right. And give _____ (name) the courage to admit, "I am hurting," yet also to release the offense against her/him. Help _____ (name) to let go perpetually and to grow from this situation. Amen.

GLOBAL CHURCH ISSUES

God of all nations, whose name and glory are manifested through all the diversity of cultures, races, and languages all around the world: We confess, O God, that even though we know you have created everyone in your own image, oftentimes our words and actions deny this truth. Help us, O Lord, truly to see your face and hear your voice through the many faces and voices of our brothers and sisters around the world.

Lord, we pray for your Church throughout the world, that amid our differences we may realize we are all parts of one body. Give us the strength to love, to listen, to hear, to share our resources, and to work alongside those who think and worship you differently, knowing that there is so much we can learn from one another and that together we can make your "Kin-dom" realized in this world. In Christ's name, we pray. Amen.

HOMELESSNESS

God who traveled in our behalf, be with your servant _____ (name), who traveled in our behalf to join us here. Thank you for the love you have shown us in our time with _____ (name), for we are always blessed when your beloved come to us. Holy Spirit, Hedge of Protection, Comforter, walk with _____ (name), stand guard over her/him as she/he sleeps and bless her/his steps as she/he wakes to go where you call her/him. God, when hope is wearing thin, stand with _____ (name). Wherever she/he goes, stay with her/him, for we know that wherever she/he is, she/he will always be within the reach of your voice, your grace, and your love. And we pray that _____ (name) might come back safely to meet us again.

Further, loving God, we pray for our world and our culture. We ask that you would continue to knit us into relationship with one another, that we might bear each other's burdens, comfort each other's sorrows, and celebrate each other's joys. Jesus, we know that we are more whole when we stand with each other. Strengthen us to do just that when seasons are hard. We trust that we are yours. May we practice the unity of sisterhood and brotherhood together all our lives long—in this place and beyond it. Amen.